JOJOBA

New Crop for Arid Lands,
New Raw Material for Industry

Report of an Ad Hoc Panel of the
Advisory Committee on Technology Innovation
Board on Science and Technology
for International Development
Office of International Affairs
National Research Council

Books for Business
New York-Hong Kong

Jojoba:
New Crop for Arid Lands, New Raw
Material for Industry

by
National Research Council

ISBN: 0-89499-188-4

Copyright © 2002 by Books for Business

Reprinted from the 1985 edition

Books for Business
New York - Hong Kong
http://www.BusinessBooksInternational.com

All rights reserved, including the right to reproduce
this book, or portions thereof, in any form.

Panel on Jojoba

NORMAN BORLAUG, Distinguished Professor of Agricultural Science at Texas A&M University, College Station, Texas; former Director, Centro Internacional de Mejoramiento de Maiz y Trigo, Mexico City, Mexico, *Chairman*

A. RICHARD BALDWIN, Director of Research, Cargill Inc., Minneapolis, Minnesota

RONALD ESTEFAN, Manager, Lubricants Evaluation Laboratory, Southwest Research Institute, San Antonio, Texas

MILTON HARRIS, Former Chairman of the Board of the American Chemical Society; former Vice President and Director of Research of the Gillette Company, Boston, Massachusetts

DONALD L. PLUCKNETT, Science Advisor, Consultative Group on International Agricultural Research, The World Bank, Washington, D.C.

* * *

NOEL D. VIETMEYER, Professional Associate, Board on Science and Technology for International Development, *Jojoba Study Director*

National Research Council Staff

F.R. RUSKIN, *BOSTID Editor*
MARY JANE ENGQUIST, *Staff Associate*
MEDGE REYES CANSECO, *Administrative Secretary*
CONSTANCE REGES, *Administrative Secretary*
RITA ROACHE, *Administrative Secretary*

During the final stages of preparation, we were saddened to learn of the death of Professor Demetrios "Jim" Yermanos, one of the most distinguished scientists working in jojoba research. His buoyant sense of optimism about jojoba generated enormous interest in the plant in Southern California and around the world. His vast knowledge of the plant, and his willingness to share that knowledge, were of immense help in the development of this book.

Preface

In 1975, the National Research Council published *Products from Jojoba: A Promising New Crop for Arid Lands,* and in 1977, *Jojoba: Feasibility for Cultivation on Indian Reservations in the Sonoran Desert Region.* Both reports drew attention to a then barely known crop called jojoba.

The aim of this present report is to review the current status of the plant, which is now fast progressing from its wild state to commercial production of impressive magnitude. In particular, the intention is to highlight the uncertainties inherent in growing and selling a new farm product. This is not to dampen enthusiasm for a crop that has truly exciting promise, but to point out unresolved questions, so that farmers and investors can appreciate the economic risks and researchers can determine where their knowledge and talents can best be applied.

It is now clear that this wild desert plant can be commercially cultivated. On sites where it is adapted, it will flower, and it will set its seed in plantations. But survival is not enough; the plants must produce yields that can be harvested and sold at a profit. This is where the uncertainty lies.

Even in commerce, however, jojoba has made a promising start. Since 1982, mounting numbers of farmers in Arizona, California, Israel, and northern Mexico have obtained commercial harvests of seed. Moreover, a number of brokers and small companies have sold increasing amounts of jojoba oil harvested from both wild stands and plantations. Present world production of jojoba oil amounts to only a few hundred tons per year, but by the 1986 season, plantations could produce one million pounds (450,000 kg) of oil. And that may double in 1987.

The development of jojoba has not always been smooth. In various parts of the world there have been high-pressure promotions and sales of inappropriate sites as quality jojoba land. The exaggerated claims of a few unscrupulous promoters have caused some people to view the plant with skepticism and have cast doubt upon the industry's integrity. It is the goal of this book to provide balanced, unbiased information.

The panel that produced this report met at Riverside, California, and Tucson, Arizona, in July 1982. The members visited commercial jojoba plantations at Desert Center, California, and Hyder, Arizona. Their initial observations were followed by extended staff investigations. The panel wishes to express its appreciation to Peter Childs, LeMoyne Hogan, William Miller, Daniel Murray, and the late Demetrios Yermanos for arranging meetings and details of the visits. Thanks are also due the contributors (see Appendix C) who provided information and reviewed parts of the text.

This report has been produced under the auspices of the Advisory Committee on Technology Innovation (ACTI) of the Board on Science and Technology for International Development, National Research Council. ACTI is mandated to assess innovative scientific and technological advances, with particular emphasis on those appropriate for developing countries.

Program costs for this study were provided by the William H. Donner Foundation. Staff support was provided by the Office of the Science Advisor, Agency for International Development, under Grant Number DAN-5538-G-SS-1023-00.

How to cite this report:
National Research Council. 1985. *Jojoba: New Crop for Arid Lands, New Material for Industry*. National Academy Press, Washington, D.C.

Contents

1	Introduction and Summary	1
2	The Plant	13
3	Production	25
4	Jojoba Oil	37
5	Uses	47
6	Markets	59
7	Commercial Uncertainties	64
8	Jojoba Industry Needs	71
9	Research Needs	74

APPENDIXES

A	Jojoba Outside North America	81
B	Sources for More Information	93
C	Contributors to the Study	98

Advisory Committee on Technology Innovation 101
Board on Science and Technology for International Development 101

JOJOBA

New Crop for Arid Lands,
New Raw Material for Industry

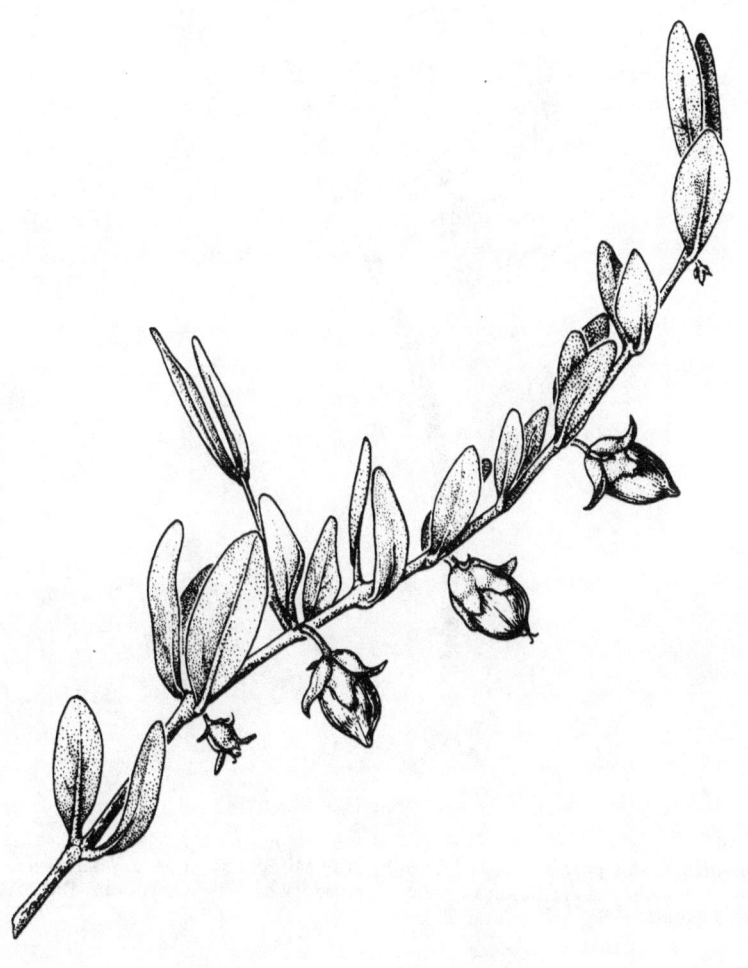

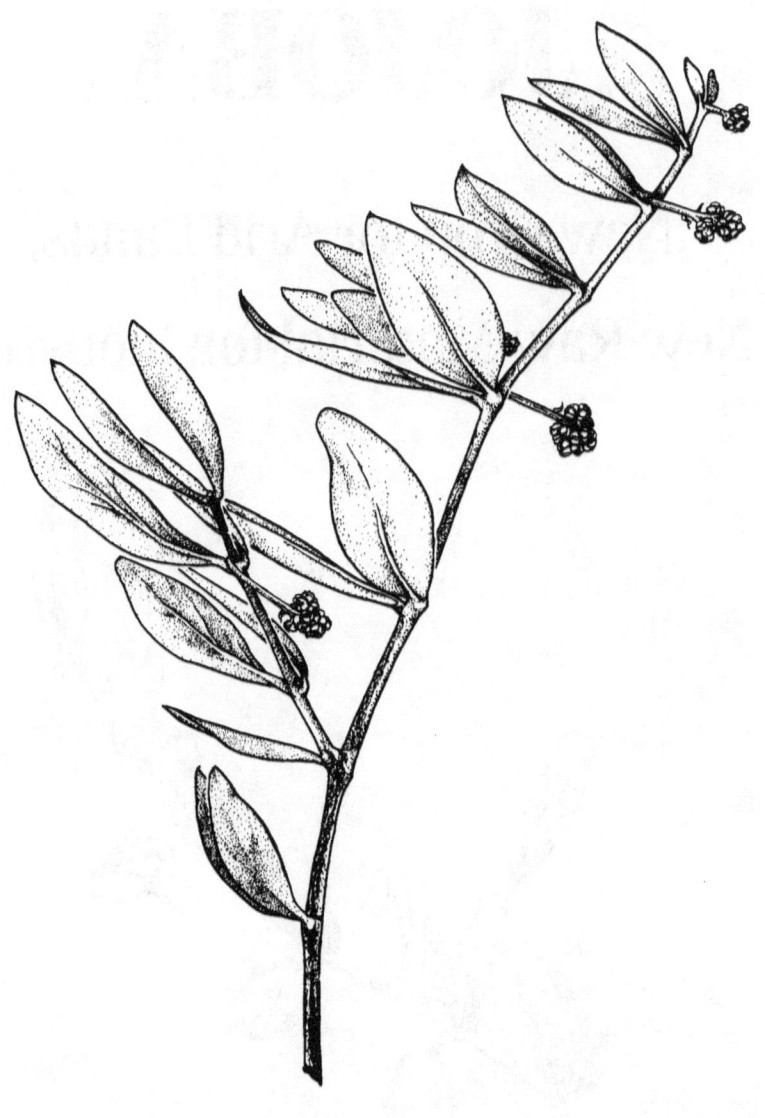

The drawings on this page and page IX are by Kay Mirocha. Source: *Jojoba: Guide to the Literature*, Office of Arid Lands Studies, University of Arizona, Tucson. © Arizona Board of Regents, 1982.

1
Introduction and Summary

A decade ago few could pronounce it, and today it still causes confusion, but jojoba (pronounced ho-*ho*-ba) is a name that is becoming increasingly common. At present, growers are attempting to produce this obscure desert shrub on about 40,000 acres (16,000 hectares) of semiarid land in the southwestern United States and in many other areas, including Mexico, parts of Latin America, Israel, South Africa, several other African nations, and Australia. Plantings in the United States alone increased 60 percent between 1982 and 1984 and represent about 32-48 million shrubs—an investment of perhaps $200 million.

For a slow-growing, perennial crop that was unknown to commercial agriculture as recently as 10 years ago, operations and investments of this magnitude are unusual and possibly unwise, but jojoba's seeds contain an oil, unique in the vegetable kingdom, that seems to have exceptional commercial promise.

Jojoba oil, which makes up about half the weight of the seeds, differs so fundamentally from common vegetable oils and animal fats that it has its own distinct characteristics. Its chemical structure is that of a long straight-chain ester, whereas the others are triglycerides—branched esters based on the molecule glycerol. Chemists call it a liquid wax.

If jojoba seed is mature and dry and the processing is done appropriately the extracted oil is remarkably clean. It has few impurities, a precise and narrow range of carbon chain lengths, and a uniform number of double bonds (one in each end of its molecule). It has a slightly yellowish color but is easily made water-white by heating or by a simple filtration through fuller's earth.

Jojoba oil's purity, lack of odor, and resistance to rancidity make it a natural base for creams and ointments, and its initial market has been in cosmetics. But it also shows promise as a new basic feedstock for the chemical industry. Researchers in more than a dozen laboratories are acetylating, alkoxylating, epoxidizing, halogenating, hydrogenating, hydrolyzing, isomerizing, ozonizing, sulfonating, sulfurizing, sulfur-halogenating, and sulfur-phosphonating it. These transformations, collectively, yield many new chemicals with broad industrial potential.

For example, jojoba-based lubricants are particularly promising.

Well-formed, mature jojoba seeds are mahogany brown, grooved, about the size of olives, and have a thin, hard seed coat. (N. D. Vietmeyer)

Properly formulated with additives, the oil (or its sulfurized or sulfur-halogenated derivatives) has excellent lubricity and a long performance life. Moreover, derivatives of jojoba oil are thought to have possible use in the preparation of antifoaming agents, detergents, disinfectants, driers, emulsifiers, fibers, plasticizers, protective coatings, resins, and surfactants.

The process of hydrogenation converts most vegetable oils into semi-solids (for example, shortening and margarine), but it transforms jojoba oil into a white, crystalline wax. This hard solid has potential as a candle wax; a polishing wax for cars, floors, furniture, and shoes; a coating for fruits and pills; an insulation for batteries and wires; and an ingredient in chalks, crayons, and soaps. In addition, if the hydrogenation process is taken only part way it leads to a range of soft amorphous waxes that melt at different—and predictable—temperatures.

The oil's double bonds are all in the *cis*-conformation. They can, however, be chemically isomerized into the more stable *trans*-form, thereby creating another range of soft waxes that seem to have considerable commercial potential of their own.

Only in the 1970s did jojoba's broad industrial and agronomic possibilities gain public attention. Before then, a handful of researchers had undertaken basic research on the crop, but it was in 1971 that the first significant harvests were reaped in the United States. At that time

INTRODUCTION AND SUMMARY

Indians began collecting and processing seed and producing oil from their reservations in Arizona and California. The resulting evaluations stimulated many researchers and entrepreneurs to begin the arduous task of converting the plant from a wild shrub to a commercial crop. For instance, various universities, corporations, and private research laboratories in Australia, Israel, Mexico, the United States, and other countries began substantial research efforts aimed at determining jojoba's basic agronomic requirements. In a remarkably short time much was learned about the plant and its management. By 1978, several landowners were confident enough to attempt to cultivate the crop.

Today, it can be said that the plant's fundamental qualities and cultivation requirements are well on the way to being understood, and that jojoba can be successfully grown in plantations. Indeed, perhaps a hundred plantations are already beginning to yield on a commercial scale. Harvesting equipment designed for use on grapes, blueberries, and raspberries has been modified for use on the crop, and custom-designed harvesters are being developed. In addition, several small companies are commercially extracting and selling jojoba oil.

In the near future, the oil's availability is expected to increase significantly. Moreover, the costs of production will decrease as existing

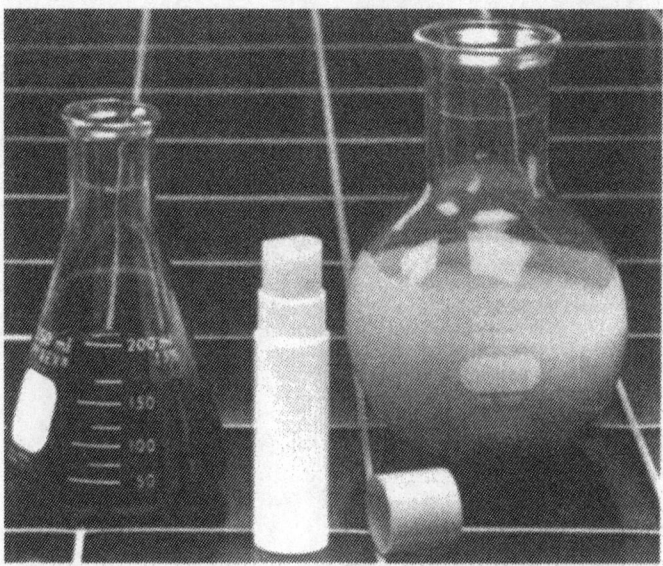

There are three main jojoba products: a liquid oil, a pastelike isomerized oil, and a hard crystalline wax. The isomerized oil differs from the natural oil only in that its double bonds are arranged differently in space (*trans* rather than *cis*). The hard wax is made by hydrogenating jojoba oil. All are unique materials never before available in quantity. (Photograph © 1985 by Kelley Dwyer, Jojoba Growers & Processors Inc.)

Desert Center, California. There are 40,000 acres (16,000 hectares) of jojoba plantations now in the United States. These are near Blythe, which is regularly the hottest place in the nation. Shade temperatures of 120°F (49°C) are routine here. Rainfall is so slight that even though 40 years have passed since General Patton trained his troops here, tank tracks are still visible. (N. D. Vietmeyer)

INTRODUCTION AND SUMMARY

Desert Center, California. Two-year-old drip-irrigated jojoba plants. Almost all U.S. jojoba plantations are irrigated. In most areas, irrigation seems to be required for the crop to produce profitable yields in a reasonable time. (N. D. Vietmeyer)

plantations mature, as extraction facilities become more efficient because of scale, and as advances in agronomy (especially the selection of high-yielding cultivars) improve yields.

This is an important and far-reaching development. Deep-rooted, long-lived perennial plants such as jojoba offer promise for agriculture in harsh, arid environments where many conventional crops cannot survive. Such woody plants with their massive root systems can extract moisture from a large volume of desert soil and can thrive where herbaceous plants shrivel to dust.

Around the world are huge tracts of semiarid land where, in principle, jojoba might become an important cash crop. It is robust, drought tolerant, and withstands desert heat without requiring much water or shade. Moreover, its water requirements are timed to meet the availability of rainfall in many deserts. For instance, it needs little water during the dry months, when water is most scarce. (Cotton,

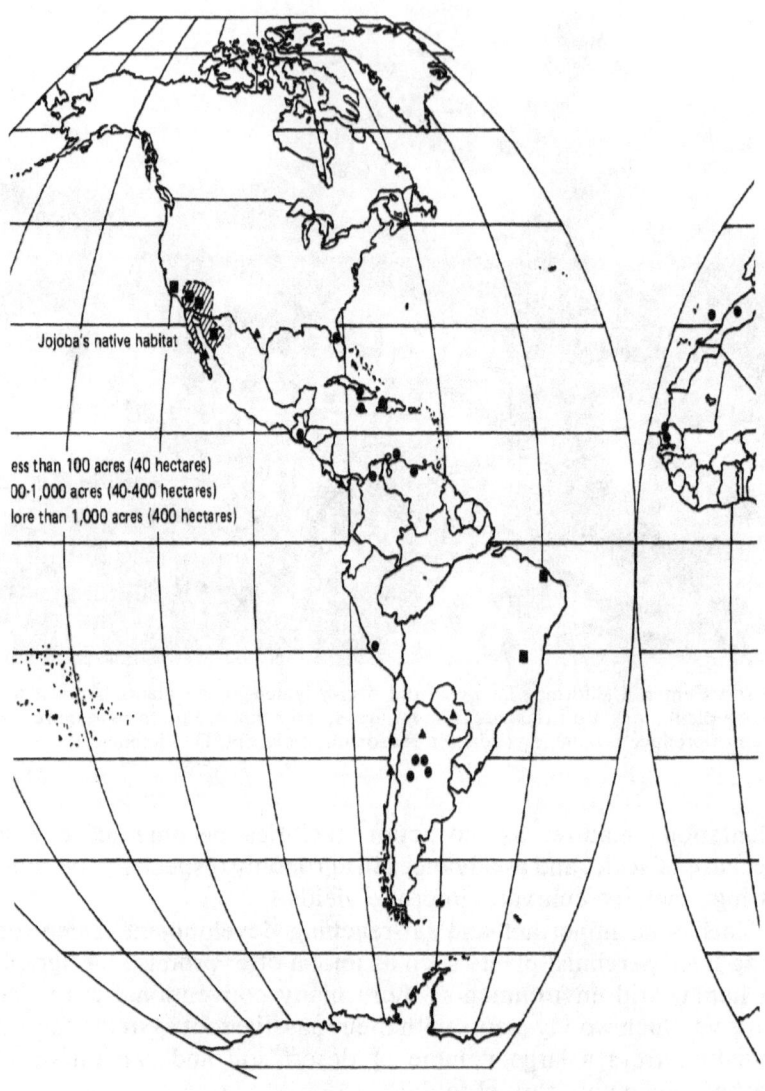

Jojoba cultivation around the world. In the last 10 years there has been a blossoming of interest in cultivating the crop, or at least in establishing a few plants as a trial.

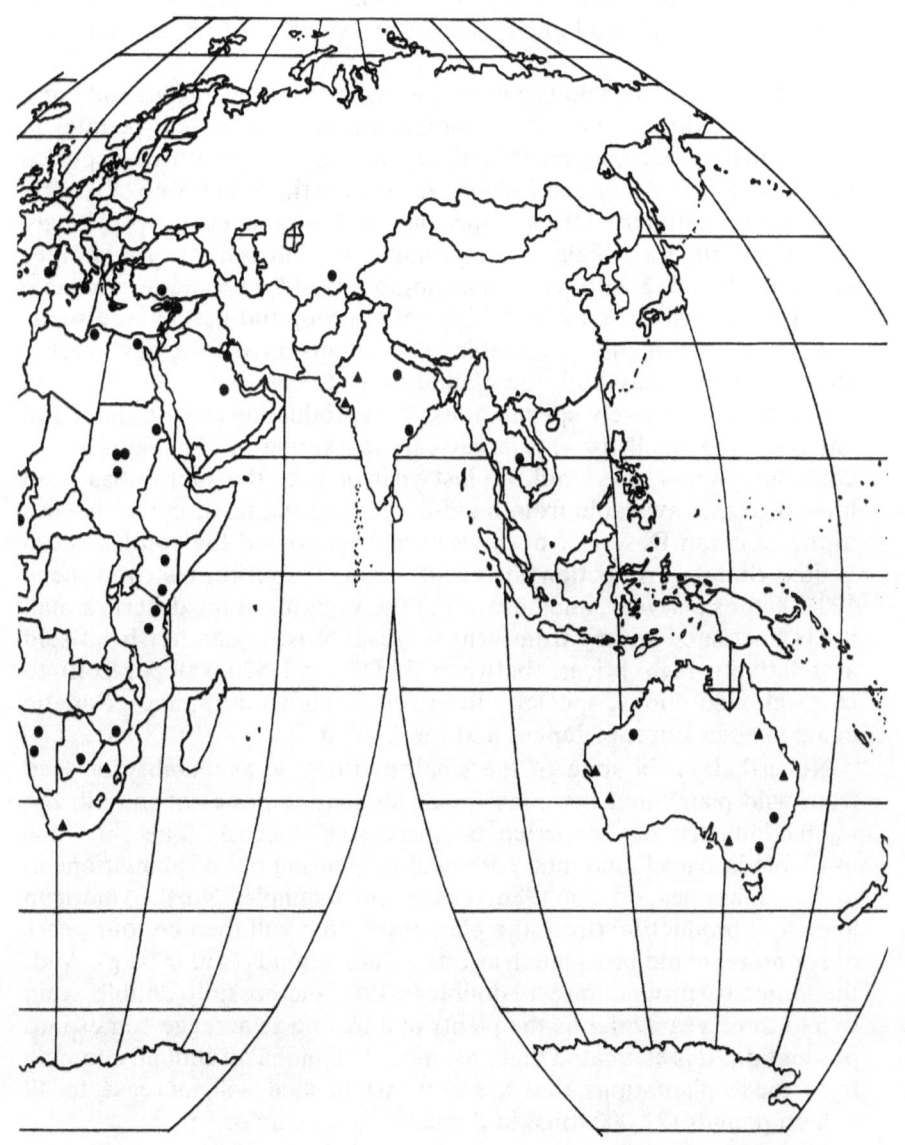

sorghum, and other crops grown in arid regions usually require irrigation during the hot, dry summer to protect them from desiccation.) Further, some types are also adapted to salinity, which is often a problem in semiarid lands.

For these reasons, jojoba cultivation and processing, the manufacture of jojoba products, and the use of by-products might help peoples in arid lands to become more self-supporting. For resource-deprived peoples—North American Indians, farmers in the Sahel zone of Africa, Bushmen in southern Africa, aborigines in Australia, peasants throughout the Middle East, Pakistan, and India, and inhabitants of arid areas in Central and South America—jojoba could become a valuable resource. It promises to be a high-value crop, and neither the seeds nor the oil are highly perishable, so that distance from the market should not seriously limit the plantation site.

But these are merely speculations. Past production around the world has been too small for any large-scale marketing of consumer goods containing jojoba oil. Until the last year or two, the supply has been limited to that available from hand-harvesting scattered native bushes in the Sonoran Desert of northwestern Mexico and the southwestern United States. Production in recent years, therefore, has only been 100-300 tons per year, and because of the vagaries of the desert rainfall it has fluctuated widely from year to year. Most jojoba has been sold at relatively high prices (between $3,000 and $20,000 per ton) to research institutions, specialty lubricant manufacturers, and cosmetic companies in Europe, Japan, and the United States.

Nevertheless, in spite of the small and erratic availability of seed from wild plants and the consequent fluctuating prices of the oil, the jojoba industry has experienced increasing success. The oil, now available in barrel amounts, soon will be pouring out of plantations in tanker quantities. In the 1986 season, for example, North American jojoba oil production (from the plantations that will then be four years old or more) could be as much as one million pounds (450,000 kg). And, theoretically, production will double in 1987 and possibly double again two to three years later as the plants mature and as acreage comes into production. It is estimated that the amount of jojoba oil annually coming from those plantations that are now established will increase to 42 million pounds (21,000 tons) in the next eight years or so.

The small cosmetic companies that initially bought jojoba oil often added it to their products for its "fashionable" value more than anything else. However, with the development of commercial plantations and the availability of experienced oilseed processors, the larger cosmetic manufacturers are beginning to add jojoba oil to their products based on its functional value. Companies such as Alberto-Culver, Fabergé, Plough-Coppertone, L'Oreal, Shiseido (Japan), and Crabtree

Jojoba oil extraction and processing facility, Apache Junction, Arizona. The crop is moving into production and several commercial facilities in Arizona and Mexico crush the seeds and sell jojoba oil and other jojoba products to industrial users. (K. Dwyer)

and Evelyn are already using jojoba oil in sun-, skin-, and lip-care products, often without advertising the fact.

In research laboratories around the world, jojoba oil is being investigated for use as a treatment for burns, acne, and psoriasis. Some research is also being conducted to test its use in processed foods. Because of its unusual molecular structure, the oil is a possible low-calorie substitute for conventional food oils, as well as a possible cholesterol-reducing agent. These dermatological and food applications are interesting but highly conjectural possibilities that require much additional study (as well as eventual approval by the U.S. Food and Drug Administration and similar agencies) before they can safely be applied.

The oil's use in lubricants and other industrial products, however, is much more certain. These applications have in the past been severely limited by the small quantity of oil available as well as by uncertainties in price. Nevertheless, two small California specialty-lubricant manufacturers, Wynn Oil and Key Oil, already use jojoba oil as lubricant additives. Among large corporations, Tenneco West has evaluated and formulated jojoba-based lubricants, and some well-known companies in the chemical, oil, and lubricants industries have tested the oil and have expressed an interest in incorporating it into various products when supplies increase and prices decrease.

Cautions

Although there are economic risks involved in farming any crop, they increase considerably when it has not been cultivated before. Jojoba, therefore, is not for amateurs or disinterested investors. To pioneer the production of such an untested plant takes dedication, commitment, hard work, and financial reserves. There have already been some financial failures. However, no crop is immune from that, and analysis shows that the failures were caused by inept management, undercapitalization, or poor choice of site, not by any major problem inherent in the plant itself.

Nonetheless, jojoba is a crop for which time-tested advice cannot be given. To manage it in plantations does not require new agricultural techniques or specialized equipment, but it is expensive, and on many sites some irrigation is required to make it profitable. So far, no significant diseases or pests have seriously affected the plant, but growers find themselves constantly battling weeds, and it seems probable that other pests and diseases will soon appear.

Also, although the main factors affecting plant production are fairly well established, many subtle factors result in economic uncertainties. For instance, the genetic improvement is in its early stages and there are essentially no named varieties or cultivars of jojoba. Thus the performance of any plant cannot be predicted or relied upon. Today's specimens (notably those established from seed) vary enormously in size, shape, precocity, yield, and oil content.

Further, jojoba is too new a crop for reliable yield predictions. Because there are no mature commercial plantations, all yield estimates are based on small experimental plots or, more recently, on young commercial plantations in Arizona, California, Israel, and Mexico. Such projections can be wildly inappropriate for other sites and they change yearly as more is learned about the crop and its requirements.

Productivity obviously depends on plant selection, suitability to local conditions, planting densities, and management practices. And these features are only just now being clarified. Different researchers and growers have differing opinions.

From present experience, it appears that on suitable sites jojoba plants grown from seedlings will produce a scattering of seed when three years old, a modest harvest worth picking at four years, and true on-line production from five years onward. This is a long delay for any investor to endure without a financial return. However, it is thought that in the eighth to tenth year the plants will reach essentially full maturity and maximum production, and from then on they should bear fruitfully with minimal attention for decades.

Significant laboratory research on the basic chemistry of jojoba oil and its derivatives has been completed. However, more product formulation and testing are required before large amounts of jojoba oil can be absorbed by industry. The crop is so new and the production so small that, as of 1985, its profitability and the eventual size and identity of its markets can only be surmised.

Supplies of jojoba oil will still be limited for the next few years, which will cause continued uncertainty over the size and value of markets. Industrial users need stable supplies and prices before they will even consider reformulating products.

The jojoba industry is fast moving into the production stage, and it will have to resolve these uncertainties soon. In a year or two, yields will surpass the needs of the present cosmetics markets, and jojoba producers will have to move from providing a high-priced speciality product to providing a lower-priced industrial commodity.

Because of this transition, any recently quoted prices for jojoba oil ($40-$55 per gallon in mid-1985, the equivalent of $10-$14 per liter) are misleading for the long term. In coming years the price will fall substantially, and many early investors, whose financial projections were based on the high prices, may have difficulty surviving. Eventually, to penetrate large markets such as that for lubricants, the oil's price will have to be comparable to that of competing high-quality synthetic or petroleum-based products.

The Future

Jojoba is graduating from the wild to the domestic, and its agronomic future looks more and more promising as experience is accumulated with each passing year. For example, plants with superior characteristics in plantations are being identified. This will allow future plantations to be established with specimens selected for high performance and cloned by rooted cuttings or tissue-cultured plantlets. Such vegetative propagation results in substantial gains in yields and harvestable production in three to four years, a year or two earlier than today.

With success in the plantations, the uncertainty of jojoba development has moved forward into the world of industrial chemistry and of product formulation and marketing. In many ways, the crop's future rests on the creativity of the chemical industry—on its ability to devise out of this unique natural product, never before available, new products and materials that will benefit both the crop, the chemical industry, and the consumer.

Jojoba has a good chance of being very profitable in the long run. It produces a premium oil. It grows in soils of marginal fertility, needs less water than most crops, withstands salinity, and apparently has a low fertilizer requirement. It has been unaffected by catastrophic diseases or insect pests—at least so far. It requires no specialized cultivation equipment and its oil can be extracted inexpensively with conventional machinery used for vegetable oils.

Jojoba growing is a challenging activity that carries risk, but it also carries the promise of excitement and personal satisfaction for the pioneers who are successful. Investment, therefore, should be made with extreme caution, but the indications are that this crop's long-term future could indeed be bright. It is not the miracle plant some have claimed, but neither is it a mirage. Many challenges are ahead, but none seems insurmountable, and success will provide the world with a new, renewable, natural resource that can fill many industry needs.

2
The Plant

Jojoba is native to a triangle of the Sonoran Desert whose corners are roughly Los Angeles (California), Phoenix (Arizona), and the southern tip of Baja California (Mexico). This area encompasses some of the earth's most inhospitable land: in some places rainfall is as sparse as 3 inches (8 cm) a year, and temperatures soar as high as 130°F (54°C). Few crops could survive this blistering environment, but among the rocks, gravel, and sand, jojoba endures.

The severity of its native habitat endows the plant with a rugged, robust nature. Some of the most northerly jojoba plants get snowed on in winter. Some westerly ones grow in sand dunes, often exposed to ocean spray, which few other species can survive. The easterly ones are in dry deserts where some years rain refuses to come at all.

Jojoba is a multi-stemmed shrub. Most specimens have a compact skeleton of branches with a dense head of foliage. However, types with many different forms can be found. Selecting the forms that best suit growers' needs is one of the challenges ahead for the crop. This bush has been pruned to open the base for easy harvest. (N. D. Vietmeyer)

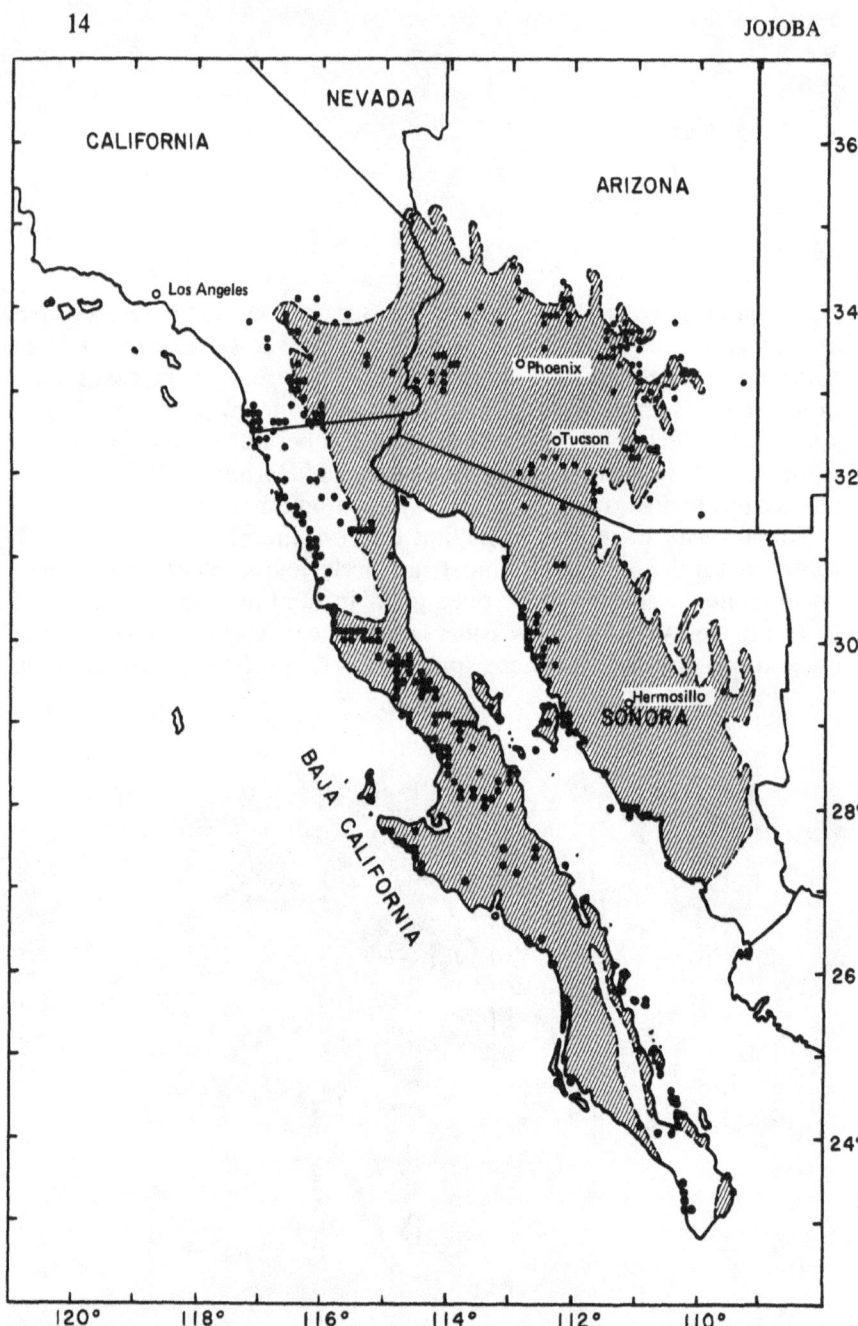

Distribution of native jojoba in the southwestern United States and northwestern Mexico. The plant occurs naturally over a range of latitudes and altitudes. It extends from the coast to inland deserts. The germplasm through much of this area still remains to be collected and evaluated. (Office of Arid Lands Studies, University of Arizona, based on an original map by R. Turner)

THE PLANT

Native stand of jojoba. The plant is "at home" in the harshness of the Sonoran Desert, which gives hope that the crop will be suitable for arid lands elsewhere. (K. Dwyer)

Appearance

Although frequently stunted to a height of 2-3 feet (60-90 cm) by the harshness of its environment or by heavy browsing by wildlife, jojoba can grow to more than 15 feet (5 m) in well-watered sites and in plantations. An evergreen, it has thick gray-green leaves and brown seed. Its natural lifespan appears to be at least 40 years. (Jojoba bushes with more than 200 rings are in fact known in the wild, although it is not known whether these represent annual rings or just growth spurts after heavy rains.)

The leaves are endowed with a dense covering of wax plates—a cuticular barrier that reduces moisture loss and protects against fungi, insects, and pollutants.

Most native jojoba plants grow among palo verde, mesquite, ocotillo, and saguaro in the desert foothills and washes. Their leaves, like soft leather ovals, stand out stiffly in pairs, creating a shield held up by a network of sturdy gray branches. Often finding little soil, they nestle together as compact spheres. On better sites, however, they resemble olive trees in their shape and color.

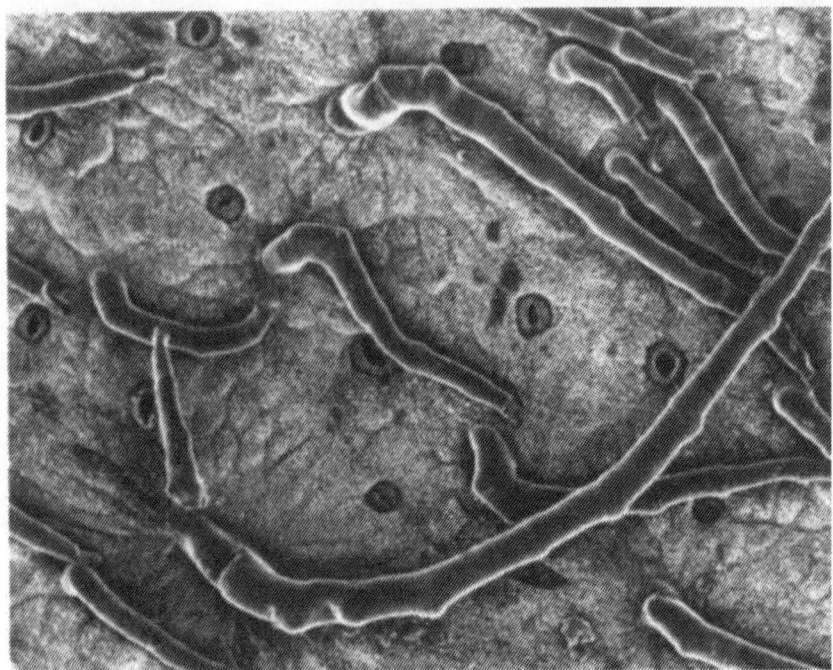

Hairs and a waxy cuticle cover the surfaces of jojoba's leaves, particularly the undersurface. The wax reduces the leaf's loss of water, serves as a waterproofing agent, and may be a sunscreen as well. Each pore (stomatum) is small and sunken and covered by a protective dome of wax and cuticle. All these features contribute to jojoba's ability to survive desiccation, heat, and sunburn. (P. Jauhar)

Taxonomy

Early in the nineteenth century, at the botanic garden of Berlin, a package of plants collected in Baja California was confused with another collected in China. When the American plants were described they were assumed to be Chinese. One, described by the garden director Johann H. F. Link in 1822, was jojoba. He named it *Buxus chinensis*.

In 1844, American botanist Thomas Nuttall described jojoba collected from San Diego. He put it in a new genus, *Simmondsia*, named to honor the English naturalist, F. W. Simmonds, a colleague who had died while studying the plants of Trinidad 18 years earlier. Nuttall's full designation was *Simmondsia californica*.

Other names and descriptions for jojoba appeared at about the same time, as well as later that century, and in 1912 the multiplicity of names was clarified by the Austrian botanist Camillo Karl Schneider. He retained Nuttall's generic name *Simmondsia* and Link's specific name *chinensis*, resulting in the full botanic epithet: *Simmondsia*

THE PLANT 17

chinensis (Link) C. K. Schneider. Despite the geographical inconsistency, this is currently jojoba's formal name.

These early botanists placed the plant in the boxwood family, Buxaceae. However, in 1898 the Belgian botanist van Tieghem suggested (on the basis of the dioecious breeding system, floral morphology, and wood anatomy) that jojoba be put into a family of its own, Simmondsiaceae. In recent times this view has been championed by several taxonomists and is beginning to gain acceptance among botanists.*

Flowers

Jojoba bushes are either male or female. The males produce pollen and have flowers containing only stamens. The females produce the fruit and seeds and have flowers containing one ovary with three ovules. Tendencies toward hermaphroditism are noted in a few male bushes. These produce all grades of perfect flowers: from those with an undeveloped pistil to those with a complete ovary that can even yield fertile seed.

The sex of a young jojoba plant cannot be judged until the first flower buds appear. In precocious individuals this may be in the summer of the first year, whereas in slow plants it may take until the fourth year.

Typically, flowering occurs at alternate nodes along the branches, although some plants produce flowers at each node and others produce them at every third node.

Male flowers occur in clusters; female flowers are commonly solitary. However, in certain populations many of the female bushes have clustered flowers. As many as 50 female flowers in a single cluster have been recorded.

Female flowers have no petals or odors to attract insects, and the plant depends almost entirely on wind for pollination. Although honey bees and a variety of other insects are often seen foraging for pollen on the male and on the hermaphroditic flowers, they rarely visit female flowers.

Floral buds appear on the current season's growth, mainly in the summer and the fall. They usually open in the following spring. This flowering is triggered by the stress of cold or drought or both. Unseasonal weather—for example, a cool fall followed by a warm, wet winter period—can trigger early flowering, which often leads to loss of the crop if the weather turns harsh.

---

* Information from R. F. Thorne.

Jojoba bushes are either male or female. Male flowers produce pollen . . .

. . . The inconspicuous female flowers are fertilized by the pollen and . . .

THE PLANT

... develop into soft green fruit (top). Over the summer, the outer skin turns brown and dries out to form a brittle, yellowish hull. Many of these hulls split (below) to expose the brown seeds inside. Most bushes hold the mature seed for several weeks, which allows time to harvest them before they fall. (K. Dwyer, N. D. Vietmeyer, and R. Schmid, respectively)

Fruiting at every node. Most female jojoba bushes produce seed at every second set of leaves. One plant in several thousand, however, produces seed at every set of leaves. This is a desirable trait that can lead to particularly high yields. (N. D. Vietmeyer)

The fruits, which are about the size of acorns, are greenish at first but turn brown as they mature, sometime during the early summer. They contain one seed, occasionally two or three. Eventually, the flesh and outer husks dry out, shrink, split, and peel back to expose the soft-skinned brown seed or seeds inside.

Roots

To help survive drought, the plants have an exceptionally deep root system that taps into the underground moisture. Bushes a mere 1–2 years old have been found with roots 12–16 feet (4–5 m) deep. Some mature shrubs have been found with roots penetrating as far as 40 feet (13 m) into the soil.

Seedlings devote most of their energy to producing a taproot—a natural survival mechanism in deserts where surface soil dries out rapidly. A seedling's taproot may grow as much as an inch (2.5 cm) a day. Often young plants have roots 10 times longer than the height of the plant above ground. Seedlings normally take about 21 days to break through the soil, by which time they can have roots 18 inches (46 cm) deep.

THE PLANT

Clusters of jojoba fruit. A few shrubs produce clusters of seed. This, too, is a rare but important phenomenon. Now that vegetative propagation is commercially possible, the cloning of such superior plants should markedly increase jojoba plantation yields. (D. M. Yermanos)

A strong taproot may be essential to jojoba's survival in many desert areas, but the plant uses water from deep soil layers only as a reservoir to resist and recover from drought stress. Some 80 percent of its feeding roots are in the top 2.5 feet (80 cm) of soil.

A symbiotic fungus, tentatively identified as *Glomus deserticola*, has been found on jojoba roots in its native state. On citrus trees, a closely related mycorrhizal fungi, *Glomus fasciculatus*, is known to stimulate the uptake of phosphorus, zinc, copper, and many other elements. The jojoba mycorrhiza probably does the same; in laboratory experiments, plants inoculated with it have experienced increased growth rates, reduced transplant shock, and heightened disease resistance.

Latitude

Natural populations occur between 23° and 35°N latitude. However, jojoba flowers and sets seed well near Fortaleza, Brazil (latitude 4°S);

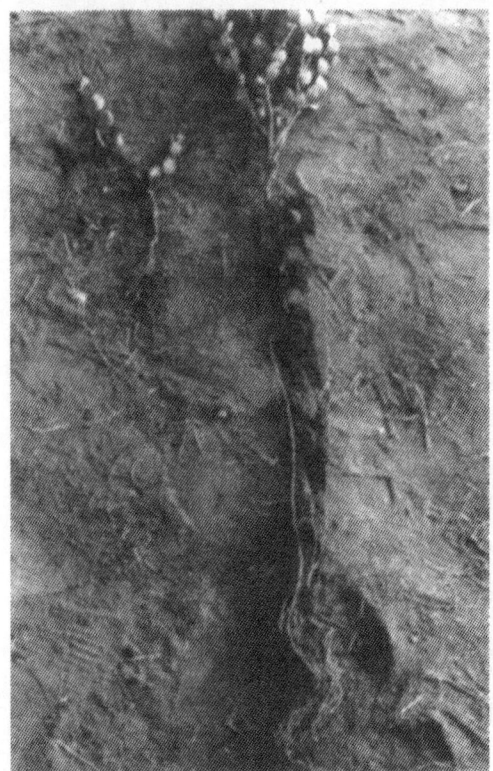

Jojoba is a taprooted plant. Each adult bush commonly has several taproots developed by repeated forking. In seedlings, the root can reach depths of 12–18 inches (30–45 cm) before the shoot even breaks the soil surface. It is an adaptation that helps a vulnerable young seedling to reach deep soil moisture before the surface dries out. (D. M. Yermanos)

Mombasa, Kenya (4°S); San Jose, Costa Rica (10°N); and Erkowit, Sudan (18°N). It would appear, therefore, that differences in latitude and daylength are not important limitations to jojoba cultivation.

Temperature

Jojoba tolerates extremely high temperatures: during the summer, daily shade readings of 95°–120°F (35°–48°C) are common in its natural habitat. Often the ambient air temperature is 120°F (48°C) and soil temperature 150°F (65°C). However, temperatures above 100°F (38°C) appear to be of no advantage to the crop, and may actually decrease its productivity because they cause the stomata to close, thereby stopping vegetative growth.

When selecting a site, it is important to consider low-temperature hazards. Aberrations in weather can cause freezes in most desert areas—on occasion. Ideally, the land should be frost free. Jojoba can grow where occasional light frosts occur, but in such areas the plants should be grown on slopes (preferably facing the sun) or where there is good air drainage. Valley bottoms where cold air collects must be avoided. Sites where temperatures frequently fall below 23°F ($-5°C$) for prolonged periods should never be planted to jojoba.

THE PLANT

Hardened plants can endure 16°F (−9°C) without sustaining long-term damage, but flower buds and any newly set seed can be damaged at 28°F (−2°C) and killed at 22°F (−6°C).

Moisture

A desert native, jojoba thrives under soil and moisture conditions unsuited to many agricultural crops. Most natural stands grow in areas receiving 8–18 inches (200–460 mm) of annual precipitation. However, although it has been called "the plant that doesn't get thirsty," it does require moderate amounts of water for quick plantation establishment and for best yields. In addition, soil moisture is critical from spring to early summer, the period in which flowering and fruit development occur.

For economic reasons, 18–24 inches (460–610 mm) of annual moisture appears to be most suitable for establishing plantations, and, in most areas, is probably needed to ensure commercial success. However, where drainage is good, extra water may not be detrimental: jojoba has been observed growing satisfactorily in sand where rainfall is 50 inches (1,270 mm) annually.

Wherever the plant is grown, good drainage is vital; jojoba cannot survive waterlogging. Flooding twice destroyed test plots near Yuma, Arizona, and most plants were killed when a test plot in Western Australia was flooded for less than two days. Losing an established plantation would be a financial catastrophe, so the possibility of a "freak" or "100-year" flood should be considered when choosing a plantation site.

Jojoba's native habitat covers areas where the main rainy seasons are in winter and/or summer. There seems to be no difficulty growing the crop in other regions that display either pattern. For example, jojoba is developing well in both the eastern (summer rainfall) and western (winter rainfall) parts of Australia. Mombasa, Kenya, gets two monsoons a year, and four-year-old plants there flower twice a year, each time following the rains.

Soil

In the Sonoran Desert, the biggest and most vigorous jojoba plants are on sloping, well-drained soils with silt and clay in the lower horizon. In cultivated stands, some plants are successful on sandy soils, others on silt-loam. Heavy clays may be suitable in some areas, but only if internal drainage is high. The plant cannot withstand soils with poor porosity. For instance, heavy bottomland soils prone to flooding are not suited to it.

Extensive measurements made in wild jojoba populations in Mexico and the United States have shown the plant thriving in soils ranging from pH 5 to 8, indicating that, within reason, soil acidity or alkalinity is probably not a limiting factor.

Salinity

The buildup of salt—because of excessive irrigation and high surface temperatures—is a common problem of arid lands. Jojoba tolerates water of low quality, provided its application is wisely managed and the soil drainage is adequate. In California, plants are growing satisfactorily with water containing 2,000 parts per million of salts. In one large planting by the Salton Sea, young seedlings are growing without obvious sign of stress, in spite of a brackish water table just 6 feet (1.8 m) below the surface. When tested in the laboratory, one variety of jojoba showed no reduced growth of flower production at a soil-water salinity of about 7,000 ppm.* Jojoba's tolerance of saline water has also been demonstrated in Israel, for example, at the commercial and experimental plantings at Kalia, near the Dead Sea.

However, some jojoba lines apparently do not survive salt stress well because leaf damage and retarded growth have been noted in some areas. The type of salt appears to be more significant than the amount: high sodium adsorption ratios (SAR) should be avoided or need to be carefully managed. Further, long-term tolerance to salinity in plantations has not been demonstrated. Salinity buildup in the root zone could be a future problem for plantations with restricted drainage that use saline water.

---

* Information from D. M. Yermanos.

3
Production

Plantations are often established in raw desert or abandoned agricultural land. To prepare the site, a source of water is first assured and the land then cleared of vegetation. The soil is ripped, plowed, disked, or land-planed prior to planting. In the United States it is often leveled (with surveying assisted by laser) or furrowed, as needed, for irrigation. Access roads may also have to be constructed, ditches dug, and fencing erected. In areas subject to flash flooding, dikes may have to be built to deflect runoff.

Plantation Establishment

Plantations are created using seeds, seedlings, rooted cuttings, or plantlets produced from tissue culture.

Direct Seeding. Most direct-seeded commercial jojoba fields are grown in raised beds. The seedbed is prepared (often using commercially available planters) as if for planting cotton or corn. In Arizona, experience has shown that with two planters mounted on a tool bar, one tractor operator can plant 60 acres (24 hectares) a day.

Jojoba seed varies greatly in size. One pound (450 g) of large seeds may number 300; one pound of small ones may contain 1,000 or more. Normally, large seed is preferred for planting because it produces more-vigorous seedlings during the first 2–3 months of growth. Most seeds, if properly handled, are 90–95 percent fertile. In cool, dry storage they remain viable enough for planting for 5 years or more.

Plantings are best done during the warmth of late spring or early fall. When soil temperatures are between 70°F (21°C) and 95°F (35°C), germination occurs within a week and the plants emerge above ground in about 20 days. Low temperatures delay germination, sometimes as much as several months, and may cause complete failure if the seed rots before germination can occur. Also, planting should be avoided during the hottest months.

During the first 2–3 months, irrigation must be applied constantly to maintain moisture near the soil surface, thereby ensuring good root establishment. Later, irrigation may be employed at monthly intervals

Hyder, Arizona. Jojoba is a new addition to world agriculture. The first commercial harvest of plantation-grown seeds was reaped as recently as July 1982. These seeds were hand harvested from plants 3–3.5 years old. Yields of clean dry seed were 30–40 pounds per acre (30–40 kg per hectare). By the time the plantations are mature the yields are expected to increase almost a hundredfold. (N. D. Vietmeyer)

to supply the field with a total of about 1.5 acre-feet (45 hectare-cm) of water. Overwatering can be disastrous.

About half the seeds produce male plants. Once these can be identified, farmers usually cut most of them out, leaving a scattering of a few strong, healthy ones for pollination. This makes room for the female bushes to grow bigger.

Seedling Transplants. To produce a seedling that is suitable for transplanting takes from 2 to 4 months in the nursery. Containers are at least 8 inches (20 cm) deep. The media is well drained and sterile to avoid fungal root diseases. Air-pruning of the vigorous taproots helps avoid the problem of the roots curling around and around in the container and refusing to grow downwards when planted out.

Where winters are cool, transplanting to the field is best done in spring or early summer. In warmer areas the early fall may be the best. The key is to get the seedlings well established before the heat of summer or the cold of winter.

Cuttings. In the United States, most jojoba plantings are currently done with cuttings. These are taken from superior bearing plants in cultivation or in the wild. Cuttings from some jojoba shrubs have demonstrated rooting rates of up to 95 percent, although this is unusual. However, many are genetically indisposed to vegetative propagation; cuttings taken from them either root poorly or fail to root at all.

Cuttings are most successfully rooted with misting techniques, using bottom heat to accelerate the process. In mist-propagation chambers kept at about 72°F (22°C), stem- and apical-wood cuttings (treated with fungicide and rooting hormone) produce roots within 3–8 weeks, depending on the season. The propagating medium is usually a mix of perlite and vermiculite. After roots have been established, the plantlets are transferred to biodegradable containers and gradually hardened off, so that planting them in the fields causes them minimum shock.

Machinery designed for planting tomato seedlings works well for planting jojoba cuttings. One grower in Arizona plants female cuttings in September or March/April and gets better than a 90-percent survival rate. He then puts cuttings of male plants into the spaces left by the females that failed to survive. Other growers plant male cuttings in a prescribed pattern from the start.

Creating a plantation by using cuttings is more expensive than by using seed. But it saves the effort and expense of roguing out and replacing unwanted plants; it gives the grower uniform plants of known sex, placement, and parentage; and it produces bushes that bear seed one or two years earlier than those from seedlings. When cuttings are cloned from superior cultivars, the yield per acre is expected to be 300–500 percent higher than that of a seed-planted field, with all its inherent genetic variability.

Cuttings are also useful for upgrading plantations that were created from seed. Replacing badly performing bushes with cuttings selected from those that perform best can more than double the overall yields.

Tissue Culture. Tissue culture techniques for propagating jojoba are available for commercial use. The economics of this procedure are uncertain, but the plantlets provide the same benefits as cuttings. Indeed, in the critical first years tissue cultured plants reportedly are the fastest growing of all planting materials.

Spacing

The optimum density for a plantation depends on the size and shape of the bushes and the management practices to be used. Time-tested

Cuttings. Thousands of select jojoba cuttings being propagated at Tucson for planting in trials in Arizona. There seems little doubt that such vegetative techniques will be used to propagate most jojoba in the future. Cuttings give growers superior plants that should boost yields severalfold; they avoid the variable stands that result from planting seeds; and they allow the male plants to be placed in the plantation in an organized pattern. Furthermore, cuttings bear seeds 1–2 years earlier than seedlings do—apparently because they are cloned from mature plants already containing the hormones that switch on flowering. (*Jojoba Happenings*)

prescriptions cannot be given at present. With more experience, a variety of densities undoubtedly will be found for different site types and cultivation practices. An acre of tall, tree-like jojobas might contain fewer than 600 plants; an acre of small bushlike ones could hold perhaps 2,000 plants. (In metric units these represent 1,500 large jojobas or 5,000 small jojobas per hectare.) University of Arizona researchers aim at a density of about 900 plants per acre (4 feet x 12 feet spacing, or 1.2 m x 3.7 m), but are testing densities up to 1,450

Tissue culture. Tissue culture technology is operational for jojoba at commercial-scale volumes. It allows mass multiplication of elite bushes—those with high yield, prolific pollen, disease resistance, or some other useful trait. It also has the ability to eliminate viral and bacterial diseases so that the plants start life in the field vigorous and healthy. Tissue cultured plantlets are produced indoors in controlled conditions, and so can be made available at any time of year. Because tissue culture produces physiologically weak roots in jojoba, the system is usually used to produce masses of shoots (microcuttings), which are then rooted in soil, just like cuttings. (H. Bollinger)

per acre (3,600 per hectare). At this time most commercial growers are working toward a density of 1,000 plants per acre (10 feet x 4 feet spacing, or 3 m x 1.2 m).

According to Israeli researchers, jojoba plants seem capable of withstanding considerable crowding without displaying depressed growth or reduced production. This is probably because jojoba has few spreading roots to compete with those of neighboring bushes. However, crowded plants may compete for deep soil moisture as they mature and the long-term effects of crowding are unknown.

Experience suggests that one male plant can provide adequate pollination for at least five female plants. Males should be spaced

Intercropping. One-year-old jojoba at Desert Center, California, with a crop of asparagus growing between the rows. The second crop shelters the young jojobas from the desiccating desert wind and from blowing sand. It also provides income to the farmer in the years during which the jojoba is maturing. Many quick-growing vegetable and grain crops seem suitable for intercropping with jojoba, but the technique demands careful management or it may adversely affect the jojoba or cost more that it saves. (N. D. Vietmeyer)

throughout the plantation with consideration given to average wind speed and direction. Recently, a computer program has been developed to help calculate the best location and spacing of males for a given site.*

Irrigation

For satisfactory growth and production, jojoba seems to need only a third (or less) of the moisture that crops such as citrus or cotton require. Nevertheless, in most places where annual rainfall is less than 25 inches (640 mm), supplementary irrigation is needed to ensure profitable production, unless the roots can reach permanent soil moisture. Supplemental irrigation can maximize production by:

- Allowing more dense plantings;
- Ensuring that the crop establishes well;

---

* Information from C. Niklas.

- Shortening the time that a young plantation takes to reach maturity;
- Doubling the number of roots;
- Increasing the bud formation in early spring; and
- Increasing the time of photosynthesis.*

For these reasons, the often-quoted statement that jojoba needs little or no irrigation can be misleading. The plants do indeed need little for survival, but economic consideration may dictate that irrigation is essential. For a healthy, profitable crop in many dry areas, extra water will be necessary.

Different methods, ranging from furrow irrigation to elaborate and expensive sprinkler systems, as well as drip or underground biwall tubes, are being used. The choice depends on the availability and cost of water, the land form, and the soil type. Normally, growers install drip and sprinkler irrigation systems on sandy soils and furrow irrigation systems on heavier soils.

The average annual irrigation applied in the United States is 2–3 acre-feet of water (50–90 cm per hectare) for established plantations and 2,000–4,000 liters per plant under drip irrigation.

Fertilization

Desert soils, particularly those used for planting jojoba, are notoriously lacking in some elements. Like all crops, jojoba needs proper nutrition, but its optimum requirements are unknown at present. However, there are indications that the plant responds to nitrogen and zinc, especially on sandy soils.† In general, though, most jojoba plantations have not been fertilized, and, so far at least, this has not obviously limited their productivity.

Intercropping

To provide income during the first few years while the plants are getting established, some growers plant another crop between the rows of jojoba. Asparagus, wheat, melon, barley, sesame, safflower, sorghum, and alfalfa have all been tried. In such cases the jojoba rows may be separated by as much as 15–24 feet (5–7 m). This reduces the amount of jojoba eventually produced, but intercropping suppresses weeds and helps protect the crop from desert winds that can literally sandblast

---

* Unirrigated plants close their stomata during the heat of the day, whereas well-irrigated plants keep their stomata open, so that irrigated plants photosynthesize for a much longer period on hot days.

† Information from W. Feldman.

Two

Jojoba "trees." Removing the axillary buds that grow into branches changes jojoba from a many-branched shrub to a treelike plant with a true trunk and a crown of foliage. (The buds are easily removed from cuttings or young seedlings with a fingernail.) Some California growers are doing this on a trial basis. It produces a plant with a clear base, which greatly simplifies harvesting and weed control. The same growers are testing the production of treelike cuttings in large containers. By forcing the growth, using fertilization and a greenhouse, the plants can reach a height of 30 inches (76 cm) in one year. At that stage they are planted out, and, reportedly, some of them begin producing seed a year after that. To compare the treelike form with jojoba's normal multi-stemmed form, see picture, page 13. (Information from R. Kadish; photo by N. D. Vietmeyer)

Unconventional Ways of Growing Jojoba

Rain-fed jojoba grown with water harvesting. Some of the finest jojoba plants in the southwestern United States are in Robert Stryker's experimental jojoba lot near Florence, Arizona. None of these is irrigated. The plantation is on sloping land and Stryker has built berms to deflect the rainfall runoff. The bushes are planted in little pits on the uphill side of the berms. This system concentrates the rainfall on the plants like a lens, and it doubles the annual rainfall of 11 inches (280 mm) that the plants would otherwise receive.

The jojoba is thriving, and such rain-fed systems hold particular promise for growing jojoba in the arid regions of the world, particularly in Third World nations with vast areas of marginal land, inexpensive labor, and little money for irrigation. (*Jojoba Happenings*)

the leaves off small tender bushes, or that can scarify leaf tissues, leaving them vulnerable to fungi and other disease organisms.

Intercropping, however, is not easy. The second crop can draw pests to, and water away from, the jojoba. So far, there have been many failures and few successes with intercropping jojoba in the United States.

Pests and Diseases

More than 100 species of insects have been identified on jojoba plants, but few cause any known economic damage. Thick hedgerows (normally an attractive habitat for insects and fungi) of jojoba have been growing for more than 14 years near Riverside, California, without requiring pesticides. On the other hand, spider mites, grasshoppers, and salt-marsh caterpillars have attacked some plants in Mesa, Arizona, and leafcutter ants have caused damage in parts of Latin America. And in 1985 a serious infestation of thrips and spider mites occurred in jojoba fields at Desert Center, California. These are ubiquitous pests, and similar attacks can be expected elsewhere.

On poorly drained, heavy soils, jojoba, like other crops, contracts waterborne fungal diseases—verticillium wilt, fusarium, pythium, and phytophthora, for example. In regions where soils drain well, this does not seem to be a problem. Fungal root diseases also can be a problem in nurseries. *Alternaria* species have been associated with jojoba, defoliating not only seedlings but also cuttings propagated under mist in greenhouses.

Wild vertebrates that may graze on jojoba foilage or fruit include birds, game animals, rabbits, and rodents. Livestock such as goats and cattle have also been known to feed on jojoba. Burrowing rodents, such as gophers, will often eat the roots. These problems can usually be reduced by fencing the fields or by setting traps.

Weeds

Weeds are the single most serious pest problem. During a plantation's early years of growth, they can be difficult to control. In the United States, Bermudagrass is one of the worst. Some growers recommend irrigating newly prepared fields to encourage the weeds to grow and then spraying herbicide before planting the jojoba crop.

The weed problem usually disappears after two years. By then, the weeds become shaded and suppressed by the growing jojoba plants.

Harvesting. Various mechanical methods are being developed to harvest the crop. Currently, it is known that the seed can either be picked from the bushes in the way blueberries, grapes, and other fruits are gathered, or can be shaken onto the ground and swept up the way almonds are gathered. It is expected that refinements in engineering design, agronomic practices, and plant selection will soon make mechanical harvesting commercially operational. (Desert Farm Management, Inc., Dateland, Arizona)

It is the between-plant weeds that are the most troublesome; weeds between the rows are easily removed by cultivation.

Timing of herbicide application is important. Care must be taken to avoid causing the flowers (both male and female) to abort.

Harvesting

Jojoba seeds are harvested when they are fully mature. Earlier harvesting reduces the quantity of wax that can be extracted and diminishes the vigor of seedlings they produce. Jojoba is nonshattering; there is enough delay between the time the seeds mature and the time they drop to allow for harvesting the crop.

In many countries, mechanical harvesting is probably essential for commercial jojoba production. In Israel and the United States, large, over-the-row jojoba pickers—modified from grape, raspberry, and blueberry pickers—have worked reasonably well. The machines use layers of plastic fingers to flip seeds off the plants and onto belts that deliver them to containers on the harvester.

These pickers have received the most attention, but machines that suck up fallen seeds from the ground are also being tested. Vacuuming can best be done if the soil lends itself to crusting. If not, a form of net may be used to catch the seed. The system has the disadvantage that the suction may pick up dirt and rocks, but it has the advantage that the seed is mature, dry, and already dehulled when it falls off naturally.

All of the seeds on a jojoba shrub do not mature at the same time, and, as of now, the bushes must be harvested more than once during the ripening season. This means harvesting costs are high and efficiencies relatively low. Costs are expected to decline and efficiency increase significantly with increased crop yields and improvements in equipment. Efforts are also underway to shorten the period of ripening by carefully controlling the timing of irrigation, by using chemicals that induce flowering, and by selecting cultivars that ripen at the same time.

Pruning

Because of their low-branching habit, jojoba bushes will require pruning before mechanical harvesters can be used. Removing basal branches can get the plant "up in the air," making it amenable to mechanical harvest, but it is not yet known whether this will reduce yields. Some farmers suggest that pruning may reduce production by 20–30 percent.

4
Jojoba Oil

In 1935, research chemists at the University of Arizona found that the oil in jojoba seeds was totally unlike that secreted by any other plant. Conventional oilseed crops, such as soybean, corn, olive, and peanut, produce glyceride oils, in which fatty acids are connected to a glycerol molecule. Jojoba oil, on the other hand, contains no glycerides or glycerol. It is composed of fatty acids connected directly to fatty alcohols.

No other plant is known to produce liquids of this type.* Jojoba apparently evolved unique enzymes and biosynthetic pathways to produce and metabolize (during seed germination) its unusual lipid. The chemical structure of the oil does not vary appreciably with plant type, growing location, soil type, rainfall, or altitude. For instance, plants throughout California and Arizona produce oil of virtually the same composition.

Most seeds contain between 45 and 55 percent oil, and average about 50 percent—more than twice the amount found in soybeans and somewhat more than in most oilseed crops. Extracting the oil is a straightforward process done with standard mechanical presses used for separating oil from peanuts, cottonseeds, soybeans, and other oilseeds. The presses extract about 76 percent of the oil in the first run and an additional 6–10 percent in a second pressing. Although all the remaining oil can be removed by solvent extraction, this is commercially impractical at present because too little seed is available to warrant its use. Experiments have shown that jojoba can also be extracted using carbon dioxide in the "supercritical process."

Physical Properties

A light-gold fluid, raw jojoba oil has few impurities, and for most purposes requires little or no refining. It contains no resins, tars, or alkaloids—and only traces of saturated wax, steroids, tocopherols,

---

* In recent years, loose claims that meadowfoam produces this kind of oil have been reported. However, it produces a glyceride oil much like rapeseed oil; to convert it into a jojobalike oil takes a series of chemical transformations.

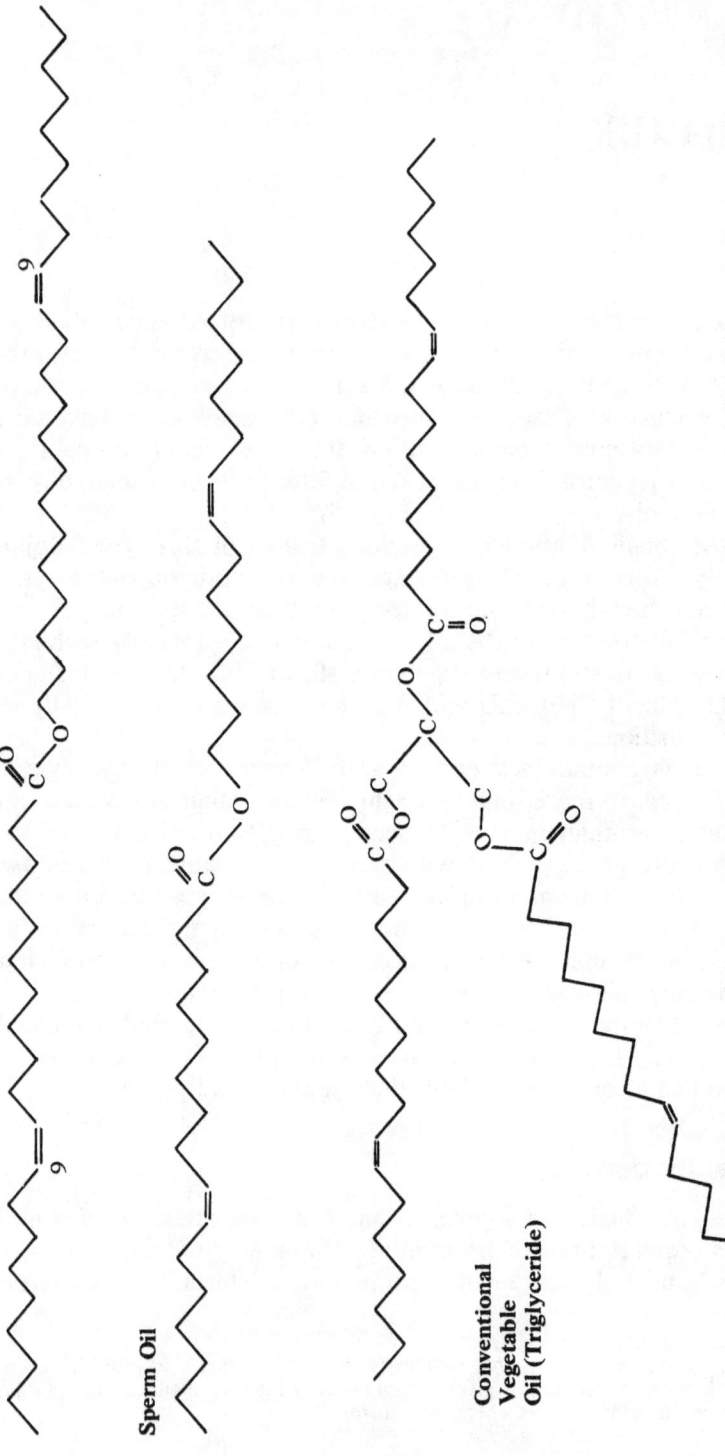

Jojoba oil's chemical structure is similar to that of sperm oil, but it is radically different from that of other vegetable oils. Of some 15,000 plant oils tested at the U.S. Department of Agriculture, only jojoba had the liquid fatty acid/fatty alcohol ester structure. The straight chain alcohols and straight chain acids that form the esters each have one double bond.

JOJOBA OIL

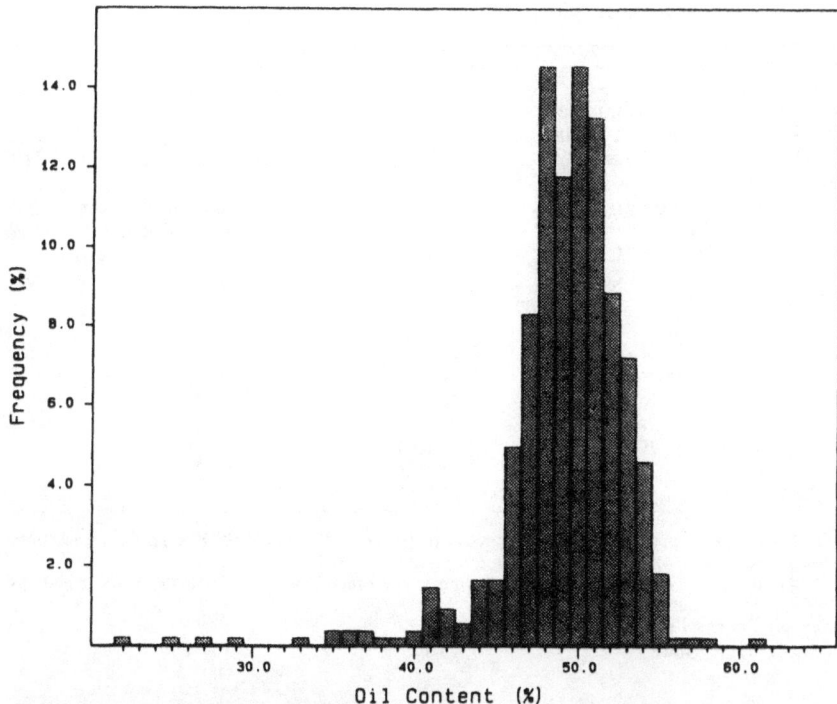

The oil content in jojoba seeds varies from less than 30 percent to more than 60 percent. Selecting plants that yield seeds with a high oil content is a target for jojoba breeders. It is not easy to accomplish because both the female bush and the pollinating plant have an effect on inducing the high-oil trait in the seeds. For this histogram, oil contents were measured by wideline nuclear magnetic resonance. This is a nondestructive technique, allowing individual high-oil seeds to be selected and then planted out. (Information from L. Anderson, R. D. Benson, and W. O'Brien)

and hydrocarbons. Neutralizing is usually unnecessary because the oil is normally low in free fatty acids. Bleaching is also usually unnecessary, but simple commercial techniques (for instance, filtration through fuller's earth) can be used to remove yellow pigments and produce a colorless product. For cosmetic and pharmaceutical use, the oil is frequently pasteurized to kill microorganisms.

Jojoba oil is easy to work with. It is nontoxic and biodegradable. It dissolves readily in common organic solvents such as benzene, petroleum ether, chloroform, carbon tetrachloride, and carbon disulfide, but it is immiscible with methanol and acetone.

For many industrial needs, the oil has promising physical properties: high viscosity index, high flash and fire points, high dielectric constant, and high stability. It has low volatility and its composition is little affected by repeated heating to remarkably high temperatures—up to 570°F (300°C), for instance.

TABLE 1 Properties of Jojoba Oil[a]

Freezing point	10.6–7.0°C	Iodine value	82
Melting point	6.8–7.0°C	Saponification value	92
Boiling point at 757 mm under N_2	398°C	Acid value	2
Smoke point (AOCS Cc 9a-48) [b]	195°C	Acetyl value	2
Flash point (AOCS Cc 9a-48) [b]	295°C	Unsaponifiable matter	51%
Fire point (COC)	338°C	Total acids	52%
Heat of fusion by differential scanning calorimetry	21 cal/g	Iodine value of alcohols	77
		Iodine value of acids	76
Refractive index at 25°C	1.4650	Average molecular weight of wax esters	606
Specific gravity, 25/25°C	0.863		
Viscosity			
Rotovisco (25°C)			
MV-1 rotor in MV cup	35 cp		
Plate and cone with Pk-1	33 cp		
Brookfield, spindle #1, 25°C	37 cp		
Cannon-Fenske, 25°C	50 cp		
Cannon-Fenske, 100°C	27 centistokes		
Saybolt, 100°F	127 SUS[c]		
Saybolt, 210°C	48 SUS[b]		

[a] Oil from expeller-pressed jojoba seeds starts to freeze at 10.6°C (51°F). It solidifies into a thick paste at 7°C. Frozen oil, allowed to warm up, melts at 7°C (45°F).
[b] Smoke and flash points determined according to the official method, Cc 9a-48, of the American Oil Chemists' Society.
[c] Saybolt Universal seconds.
SOURCE: T. K. Miwa.

Jojoba oil also has good keeping qualities and an exceptional shelf life. This is apparently due to the presence of natural antioxidants (alpha-, gamma-, and delta-tocopherols), which occur in concentrations of about 50 ppm. In practical terms, these antioxidants keep the oil from becoming rancid, and companies processing raw jojoba oil are reporting very low acid values (0.2–0.3), even without neutralization.

In one experiment, seeds analyzed 25 years after harvest showed no change in composition. It appears, therefore, that the dry seeds can be stored without deterioration or chemical changes.

Chemical Properties

For a raw natural extract, the oil is remarkable for its molecular uniformity: it is 97 percent linear wax esters. (The remainder comprises free fatty alcohols and acids, and tocopherols.) It also has an amazing internal homogeneity—more than 87 percent of the esters present are combinations of acids and alcohols with chain lengths of 20 or 22 carbon atoms. By contrast, common vegetable oils have fatty acids whose carbon chain lengths are mostly 16 and 18.

The esters are composed almost entirely of straight-chain acids and alcohols. The acids are a mixture of eicosanoic (C_{20}) and docosanoic (C_{22}), with small quantities of palmitoleic (C_{18}) and oleic (C_{16}). The

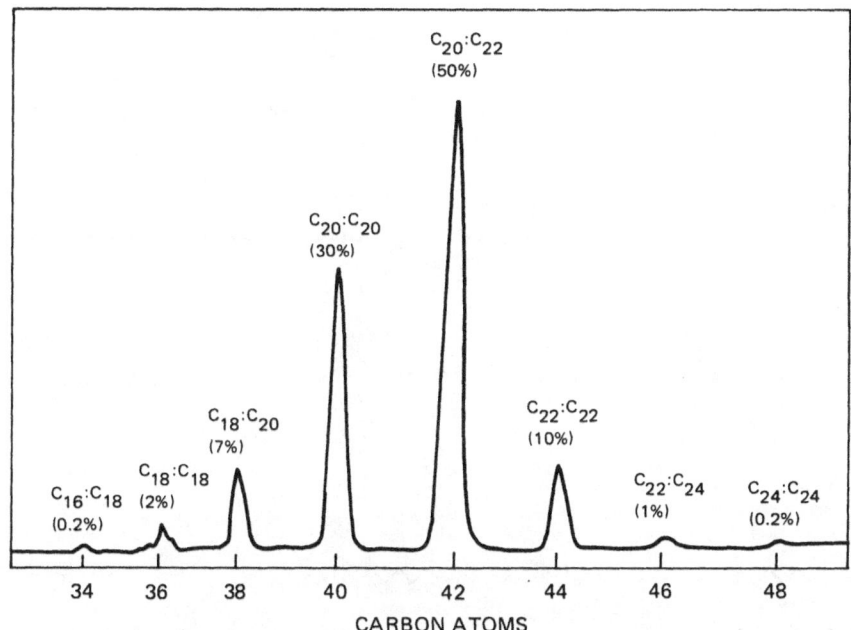

Jojoba oil esters are made up of fatty alcohols and fatty acids that are predominantly 20 or 22 carbon atoms long. Compared with most vegetable oils, the carbon chain lengths are remarkably uniform. (Information from T.K. Miwa)

alcohols are a mixture of eicosanol and docosanol, with smaller quantities of hexacosanol and alcohols of lower molecular weight.

The acids and alcohols that make up jojoba oil each have a single double bond. Moreover, all double bonds are in the ω_9 position (i.e., between carbon 9 and carbon 10, counting from the methyl end). This is a remarkable molecular purity, and the double bond position is different from that usually found in vegetable oils.

The nature of the oil can be grossly changed by reactions at the double bonds and ester functions, and many new products can result. One research laboratory in Israel, for example, has produced more than 40 different jojoba-based chemicals that appear to have commercial industrial applications.*

As in other natural oils, the double bonds in fresh jojoba oil are all in the *cis* configuration. However, they can be easily isomerized (twisted around in space), using as catalysts traces of selenium, nitrogen oxides, or active earth. This produces an equilibrium mixture with 20 percent *cis* and 80 percent *trans* double bonds. This simple process dramatically transforms the liquid into a soft, opaque cream resembling face cream. It can be stopped at various intermediate degrees of

---

* Information from A. Shani and J. Wisniak.

Jojoba oil can be transformed into a remarkable array of products. Research chemists have already produced more than 40 different compounds of potential commercial significance. . . .

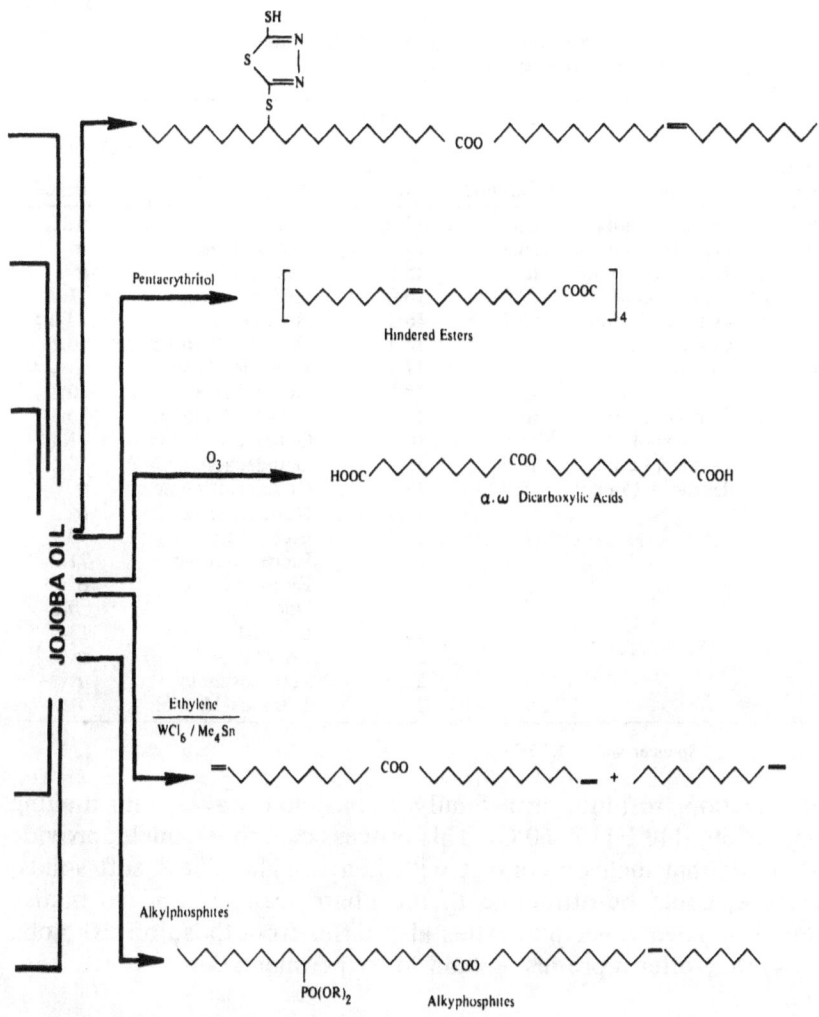

... Many of these conversions are simple, cheap, and can be readily made on an industrial scale. Once jojoba oil becomes available in quantity, it promises to be a new raw feedstock for the chemical industry. (Based on information from P. Landis, A. Shani, and J. Wisniak)

TABLE 2 Alcohol/Acid Structures of Jojoba Oil Determined by Gas Chromatography and Mass Spectrometry

Carbons and Double Bonds	Alcohol	Percent	Carbons and Double Bonds	Acids	Percent
14:0	Tetradecanol	trace	12:0	Dodecanoic	trace
16:0	Hexadecanol	0.1	14:0	Tetradecanoic	tr.
17:1	Heptadec-8-enol	tr.	15:0	Pentadecanoic	tr.
18:0	Octadecanol	0.2	16:0	Hexadecanoic	1.2
18:1	Octadec-9-enol	0.7	16:1	Hexadec-9-enoic	0.2
18:1	Octadec-11-enol	0.4	16:1	Hexadec-7-enoic	0.1
20:0	Eicosanol	tr.	17:1	Heptadecenoic	tr.
20:1	Eicos-11-enol	43.8	18:0	Octadecanoic	0.1
21:1	Hencos-12-enol	tr.	18:1	Octadec-9-enoic	10.1
22:0	Docosanol	1.0	18:1	Octadec-11-enoic	1.1
22:1	Docos-13-enol	44.9	18:2	Octadecadienoic	0.1
24:1	Tetracos-15-enol	8.9	18:3	Octadecatrienoic	tr.
			19:1	Nonadecenoic	tr.
			20:0	Eicosanoic	0.1
			20:1	Eicos-11-enoic	71.3
			20:2	Eicosadienoic	tr.
			22:0	Docosanoic	0.2
			22:1	Docos-13-enoic	13.6
			23:1	Tricosenoic	tr.
			24:0	Tetracosanoic	tr.
			24:1	Tetracos-15-enoic	1.3

SOURCE: G. F. Spencer and T. K. Miwa.

isomerization, resulting in a family of pastelike waxes with melting points of 50°–140°F (10°–60°C). This process can, for example, provide soft solids that melt on contact with human skin. These soft solids, therefore, could be attractive to the pharmaceutical and cosmetics industries. Their other properties also differ from those of *cis*-jojoba oil and they offer a promising field for experimentation.

Jojoba Wax

Hydrogenation (commercially called "hardening") is one of the most well-known transformations of fats and oils. Hardened vegetable oils are ingredients in shortening and margarine. Hardening jojoba oil through hydrogenation produces a crystalline wax.* This lustrous, pearly white, crystalline solid has properties like those of beeswax, candelilla, carnauba, and spermaceti—all of which waxes are commercially in demand and subject to steeply rising costs and uncertainties of supply.

---

* To chemists, liquid jojoba oil is also a wax and they call the hard solid "hydrogenated jojoba oil." In this report, we use the words jojoba oil and jojoba wax to distinguish the liquid from the hydrogenated solid.

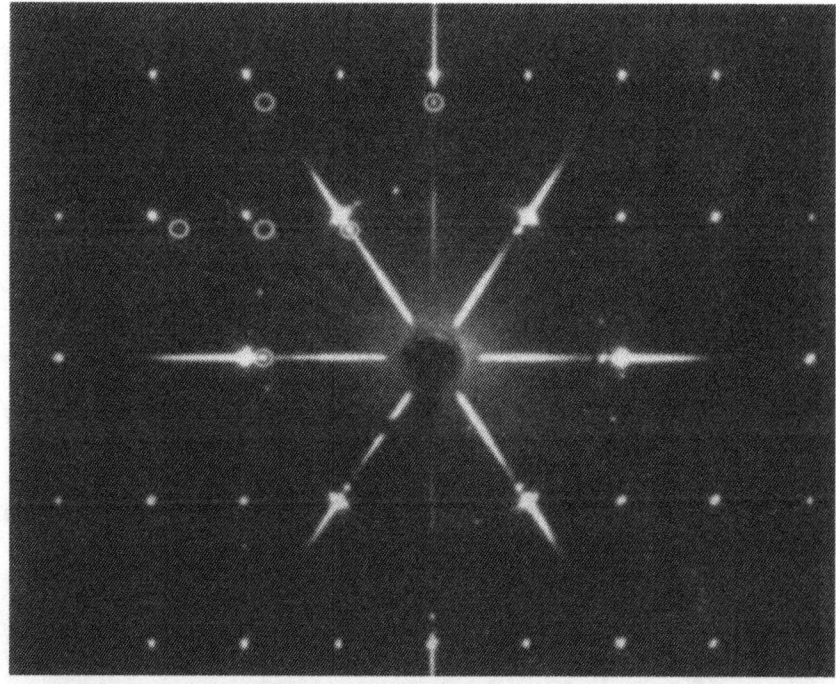

Although hydrogenation converts other vegetable oils to soft, amorphous fats such as shortening and margarine, it converts jojoba oil into a remarkable hard wax that is crystalline enough to provide an X-ray diffraction pattern. No other readily available natural wax is so crystalline. Jojoba wax, a shiny, sparkling product, is fully miscible with polyethylene, which gives hope that an array of useful slow-release products ranging from lubricants to pesticide carriers can be developed using it. (T.K. Miwa)

The hydrogenation process can be carried out with standard equipment used in the fats industry. It can be stopped part way to produce a range of soft-to-hard waxes, as desired.

Composed essentially of pure wax esters with no double bonds, jojoba wax is made up of saturated C_{20} and C_{22} fatty acids and alcohols. X-ray diffraction has shown that the ester molecules are lined up in hexagonal arrays, but the samples are not completely crystalline, probably because the slightly differing lengths of the carbon chains prohibit perfect ordering.

Jojoba wax is now available in quantities adequate for industrial purposes, and it appears to have considerable commercial promise. Hard waxes are in demand, but most are from wild species whose supplies are intermittent, haphazard, or declining. Carnauba wax, which is laboriously scraped from fronds of a palm that grows in Brazil, is in erratic and dwindling supply, and its price (fueled by greatly increased labor and transportation costs) is rising. Candelilla, another cuticular wax, is obtained by boiling the stems of a wild shrub

TABLE 3 Properties of Industrial-Grade Jojoba Oils

Typical	Pure Grade
Gardner color	Maximum—9
Odor	Typical fatty
Acid value	Less than 1.00
Saponification number	90–95
Iodine value:	80–85
Total plate count	Less than 50/gram
Melting point	7°–9°C
Flash point	295°C
Fire point:	338°C

SOURCE: T. K. Miwa.

found in Mexican deserts. Its supply, too, is uncertain, and for the same reasons. Spermaceti (the saturated form of sperm oil) was once an important hard wax, but its use in the United States and most other countries has been banned since the 1970s because of the sperm whale's endangered status.

Hardness is one of jojoba wax's most outstanding characteristics. It is harder than beeswax but is slightly softer than carnauba. In fact, the hardness (which industrial chemists register by melting point) of fully hydrogenated wax approaches that of the "king of waxes," carnauba. Its melting point is about 158°F (70°C). Although this is slightly lower than that of carnauba, it is higher than that of most other waxes. Moreover, jojoba wax is sparkling, white, and crystalline, and in many applications may be superior to the yellow amorphous waxes such as carnauba.

Because it is produced from liquid, unsaturated oil, which is more readily and cheaply purified than a solid such as carnauba, hydrogenated jojoba wax can be made exceptionally pure. Where crystallinity is a disadvantage, jojoba wax can easily be made amorphous by adulterating it with small amounts of other waxes.

Jojoba oil's double bonds offer chemical functionality that can be put to advantage to produce partially hydrogenated oils. This change produces a range of soft plastic waxes melting at temperatures up to 140°F (60°C). This offers alluring possibilities for industry because an array of soft white waxes and creams with a range of melting points can be produced to a given melting-point specification.

Jojoba wax has the capability to form a "gel" with many other chemicals. It has been found to improve the physical structure of many cosmetic products through special coupling mechanisms that allow two previously incompatible materials to be used together in the same formula.*

---

* Information from J. H. Brown.

5
Uses

Jojoba oil is unproven in wide-scale commercial practice, but it offers the chemical industry a new basic raw material that in the near future will be produced in bulk. Liquid waxes have never before been available to industry from a cultivated plant. It seems likely that, with the first significant supplies becoming available, industrial chemists will soon uncover many new and wide-ranging uses for this unique natural product.

Jojoba oil and its derivatives seem to have potential for uses in products as diverse as cosmetics, pharmaceuticals, lubricants, foods, electrical insulators, foam-control agents, high-pressure lubricants, heating oils, plasticizers, fire retardants, and transformer oils. Moreover, jojoba oil is also a source of long-chain alcohols and acids with double bonds in slightly different positions from those in other natural fatty acids.

As already noted, jojoba oil's boiling point is high—a desirable feature in many applications. In addition, the oil has thermal stability and high smoke, flash, and fire points. The decomposition point is 600°F (315°C).

On the other hand, the freezing point (45°–51°F; 7°-10.6°C) is also high, and this may limit the oil's uses. For instance, the freezing point may be too high for some lubricant or food uses where the oil could solidify in cold weather or in refrigerated products.

Lubricants

Until the early 1970s, sperm-whale oil was a common ingredient in high-quality lubricants. It was used notably in vehicle differentials and transmissions, in hydraulic fluids that need a low coefficient of friction, and in cutting and drawing oils. The high-pressure lubricants used worldwide—for example, those in most automobile transmissions—commonly contained 5–25 percent sperm oil. In some of these, unmodified sperm oil was used, but more often it was sulfurized; sometimes it was epoxidized, chlorinated, or phosphorylated before being added to the lubricant base stock.

The enactment of legislation to preserve the sperm whale banned

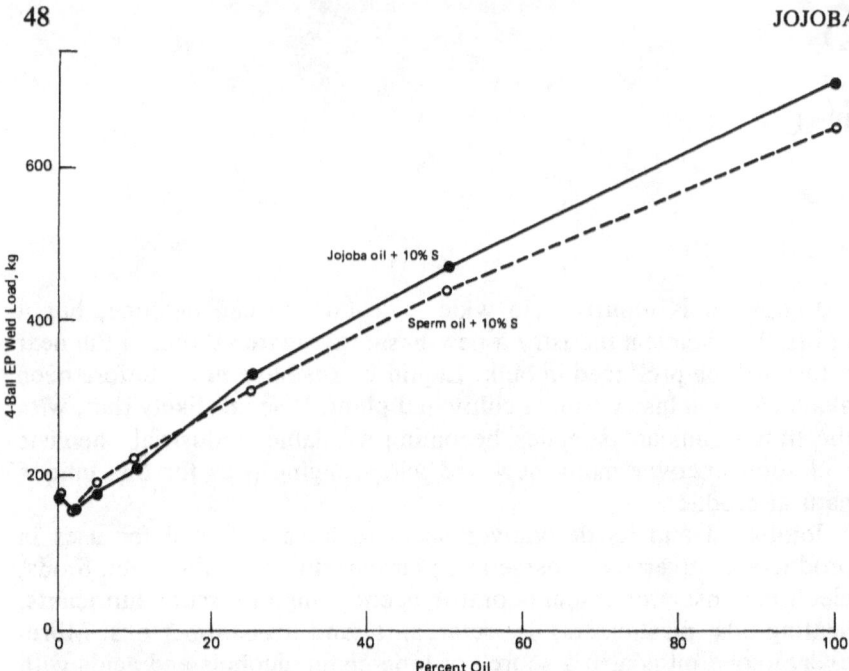

Sulfurized jojoba oil in general lubricants. Laboratory tests have demonstrated that jojoba can match the exceptional lubricating qualities of sperm oil. (Source: H. Gisser)

all these uses. However, jojoba oil's composition and physical properties are close enough to those of sperm oil to ensure its suitability as a substitute. In principle, it, too, could end up in most of the vehicle transmissions used around the world. Its oiliness and surface-wetting properties are particularly promising for extreme-pressure/extreme-temperature gear oils and greases. Its wetting properties mean reduced wear and its nondrying characteristics prevent gumming and tackiness.

Actually, jojoba oil has several advantages over sperm oil:

- It has a mild, pleasant odor, with no fishy background.
- It contains no triglycerides (sperm oil contains about 30 percent).
- It requires little or no purification.
- It can absorb larger amounts of sulfur, giving better lubrication per unit weight.
- It does not darken significantly on sulfurization.
- The highly sulfurized oil is liquid, whereas mineral oil must be added to keep sulfurized sperm oil liquid.
- It is a renewable vegetable product that can be produced without destroying an endangered species.

Incorporating sulfur or sulfur-containing compounds enormously enhances the lubrication qualities. Extensive evaluations have shown that sulfurized jojoba oil has properties equivalent to or much better

USES

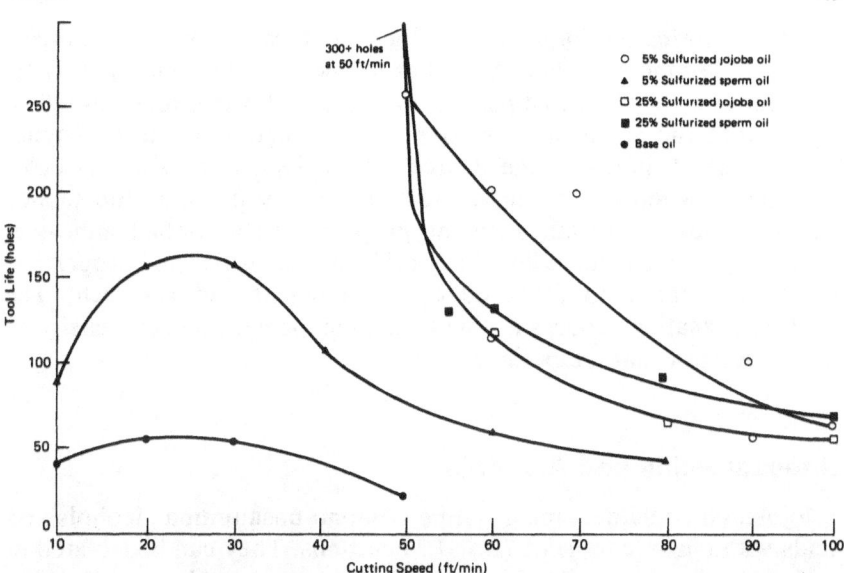

Sulfurized oil in cutting-tool lubricant. Bench tests have shown that adding sulfurized jojoba oil to a base oil dramatically improves the life and cutting speed of machine tools. (Source: J. Messina)

than sulfurized sperm oil in lubricant applications. Under extreme pressure it is at least as good at improving the antiwear properties and load-carrying capacity of both naphthenic and bright-stock base oils. In some tests, when small amounts of sulfurized jojoba oil were added to lubricants, the performance improved so much that it exceeded the limits of the testing machine.

When, in addition to sulfur, a molecule such as phosphorus, chlorine, or bromine is incorporated into the jojoba molecule, a synergistic action occurs and an even better lubricant additive is obtained. Sulfurchlorinating jojoba oil particularly enhances the wear properties, while sulfurbrominating it improves the load-carrying capacity.*

Jojoba oil's main limitation as an ingredient in lubricants is its high pour point. Below 50°F (10°C) the oil solidifies. Thus, as of now, jojoba is likely to be most useful in lubricants for use at high temperatures.

Factices and Adhesives

Vegetable oils react with sulfur chloride to form materials known as factices, which are used in manufacturing varnishes, adhesives, printing ink, and flooring materials.

---

* J. Wisniak and H. Benajahu, U.S. Patent 4.130.495 (1978).

Sulfurchlorinating jojoba oil produces an array of products ranging from oils to rubbery solids. Each has its own qualities and properties. A sulfur content of up to 4 percent produces a flowing, reddish-yellow liquid with the same pleasant odor as raw jojoba oil itself. Higher sulfur content increases the factice's viscosity and darkens its color to brown. When the sulfur content exceeds 9 percent, the factice becomes elastic and takes on the properties of a contact adhesive. This array of products, with widely differing viscosities and properties, offers an open field for product development and research. The sulfurchlorination process is simple and inexpensive and can easily be performed at room temperature.

Unusual Acids and Alcohols

Jojoba oil could become a source of mono-unsaturated alcohols and acids with chain lengths of 22 and 24 carbons. They can be isolated in unusual molecular purity. In principle, these acids and alcohols could be used as intermediates in the preparation of disinfectants, surfactants, detergents, lubricants, driers, emulsifiers, resins, plasticizers, protective coatings, fibers, and corrosion inhibitors. They might also prove valuable as bases for creams, ointments, antifoams for industrial use, and numerous other products. They have longer chain lengths than those currently available, and this makes possible a new range of materials with subtly changed properties.

Cosmetics

Olive oil, beeswax, and fats are traditional cosmetics bases, but jojoba has important aesthetic and technical qualities that could also make it a widespread basic cosmetics ingredient. Indeed, in recent trials, cosmetics researchers have found that refined jojoba oil was superior to all alternatives. It has no resins, tars, glycerides, alkaloids, glucosides, or low-molecular-weight fatty acids. And, because of its stability toward rancidity and its pleasant feel on the skin, it could become a standard oil-phase base for the cosmetics industry.

Jojoba oil has already been widely used in cosmetics in the United States and Europe. As many as 300 products have appeared in United States markets alone. But most of these have used jojoba oil only for its novelty value, not for its fundamental qualities. Such health and beauty care products have been successful largely because jojoba oil is easily substituted for other oils. But manufacturers are now coming

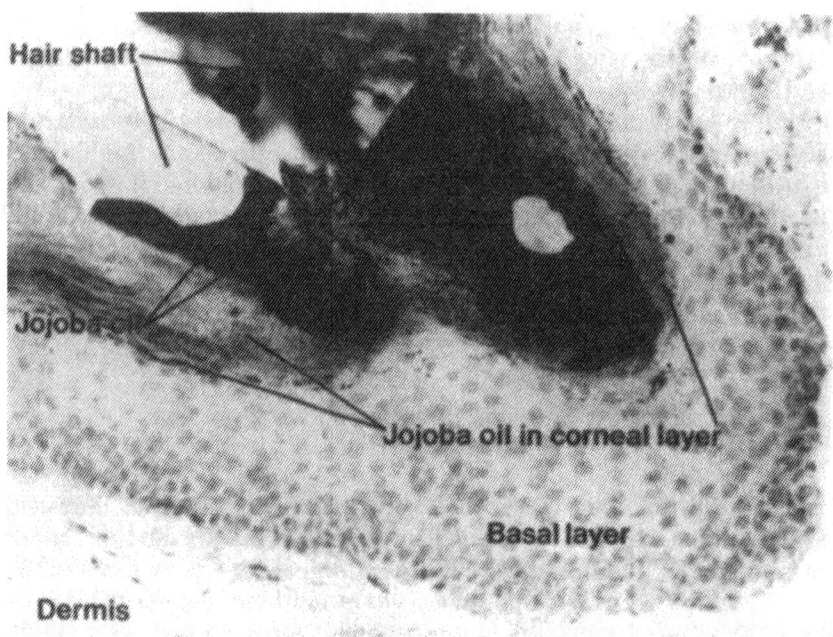

Jojoba oil penetrating skin. Experiments at the University of Michigan show that jojoba oil has an apparently unique ability to penetrate skin. Here, special stains show the oil pooled at the bottom of a hair and moving through the follicle wall into the corneal layer. This demonstrates jojoba oil's potential to soften skin from within, a property that could lead to it becoming a basic ingredient in many cosmetic products. (K. D. McClatchey)

to realize that the oil has high aesthetic qualities, better stability than even mineral oil, and lacks the problems of conventional triglyceride oils. *

Among the varied products already being sold are shampoos, hair conditioners, hair sprays, facial oils, body oils, bath oils, hand lotions, moisturizers, suntan lotions, make-up removers, shaving creams, lipsticks and lip glosses, vanishing creams, cleansing creams, and skin fresheners.

A Japanese cosmetic company (Koei Perfumery, Tokyo) has reported the absence of any acute toxicity in laboratory studies and clinical tests carried out with jojoba and jojoba-based cosmetics over a period of almost 10 years. No acute toxicity nor eye irritation resulted from use. Indeed, only 3 out of 46 persons, chosen for their susceptibility

---

* Information from H. Libby.

to dermatological problems, showed even slight irritation. Similar favorable results have been reported in toxicity studies conducted in the United States.

Skin seems to absorb jojoba oil within a few minutes, and transdermal penetration is suspected, although not yet proved. A preliminary investigation at the University of Michigan suggested that it penetrates the outer skin via hair follicles and accumulates within the keratin layer beneath. Neither triglycerides nor lanolin had this ability; the characteristic was unique to jojoba. Thus, jojoba oil promises not only to help make skin supple and smooth, but perhaps to carry medications into the skin as well.*

Preparation of Pharmaceuticals

Sperm oil has long been valued for controlling foam in industrial fermentations. It has excellent antifoam properties and is barely metabolized by the microbial cultures. Comparative tests have shown that jojoba oil could also be an excellent antifoam agent, at least for the production of penicillin G and cephalosporin. In fact, in a couple of experiments, the yield of penicillin unexpectedly increased by more than 20 percent when jojoba oil was substituted for sperm oil. The results have been so satisfying that industry sources have indicated they would switch entirely to jojoba if sufficient supplies could be assured.† More research is needed to settle the matter, however, because experiments in Israel found that jojoba oil was ineffective in foam control in other applications.‡

Medicinal Uses

Jojoba oil may have potential as a treatment for skin disorders. At the Ben-Gurion University Hospital in Beer-Sheva, Israel, 35 patients with severe acne were treated with cream containing jojoba oil. Doctors conducting the test report that the patients found it pleasant to use, and it seemed to ease their conditions in all cases. There were no side effects, and it restored a natural shine to skin. However, although it

---

* Information from K. McLatchey.
† Information from S. G. Pathak.
‡ Information from J. Wisniak.

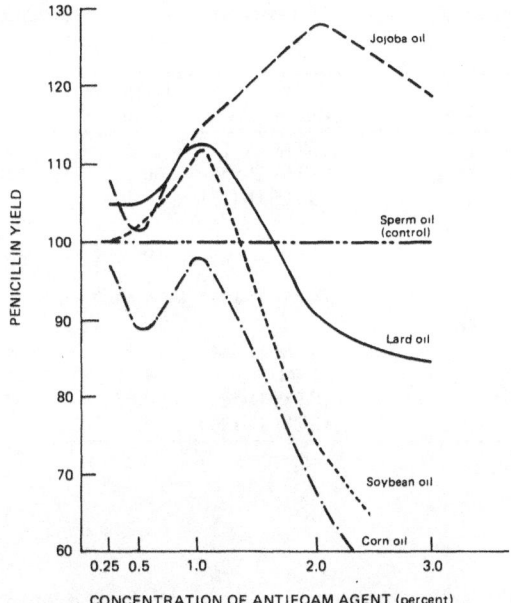

Jojoba oil seems to have promise for use as an antifoaming agent in fermentation processes. Shown are the results of a set of experiments on the formation of oral penicillin. Various vegetable oils were used in various concentrations to break the foam in the fermentation flasks, and the penicillin production was measured against that resulting when sperm oil was the antifoam. Because sperm oil has long been the standard antifoam used by the pharmaceutical industry, it was surprising that substituting jojoba oil increased the penicillin yields dramatically. If such findings hold up in production scale, the increased yield would be a financial boon to the pharmaceutical industry. (Information from S. G. Pathak)

slowed down the acne outbreaks, it did not stop the eruption of new pustules.*

At the same university, 27 patients with psoriasis were also treated with jojoba oil-based creams. These, too, were well accepted and some noticeable improvement in skin condition was recorded. Psoriasis medicines today are either unpleasant black mixtures of coal tar and mineral oil or expensive steroids with unpleasant side effects, so this may prove to be a promising line of research.

Dermatological research suggests that jojoba oil may help reduce inflammation.† And in Israel, 40 volunteers in a laboratory used a jojoba cream for sunburn and chapped hands. There were no allergic reactions and the users reported getting relief.

---

* Information from B. Mosovich.
†Information from K. McLatchey.

TABLE 4 Comparison Between Hydrogenated Jojoba Oil, Beeswax, and Carnauba Wax

Property	Unit	Method	Jojoba Wax (White)	Beeswax	Carnauba Wax
Melting point	(°C)	ASTM D-127	67.0	64.0	75.5
Congealing point	(°C)	ASTM D-938	66.5	62.0	68.9
Penetration	$\left(\frac{1}{10}\,mm\right)$	ASTM D-1321			
at 77°F			6	20	9
at 100°F			7	41	13
Refractive index at 80°C	(n_D^{80})	ASTM D-1747	1.4380	1.4400	1.4361
Total acid no.	(mg KOH/g)	ASTM D-664	1.9	18.4	3.3
Iodine value	(g/100g)	1.P.84	4	12	3
Ash	(% wt)	ASTM D-482	0.02	0.001	0.02
Color		ASTM D-1500	L 0.5	L 1.5	1.0

SOURCE: T. K. Miwa

Foods

Jojoba oil's use as a possible cooking oil has often been speculated about. It has desirable culinary properties. It is stable, bland tasting, and has no unpleasant texture. Its unusual chemical structure could make it resistant to hydrolysis by the digestive enzymes that hydrolyze most fats. Thus, the oil would be digested much less than conventional lipids, perhaps making it healthful, low-calorie food oil. (The undigested portion is eliminated in the feces.)

The Nestlé Company in Switzerland has shown that laboratory rats have no dislike for, or reluctance to eat, jojoba oil. The rats ate the same amount of food as the control. It lowered their body weights and the animals were lean at the end:

These results indicate that jojoba oil may well be marketable as an edible oil for dieters. Much costly research will be needed, however, to prove its effectiveness and safety, and official acceptance from regulatory agencies will be necessary as well.

Other Uses of Jojoba Oil

Jojoba oil is highly resistant to rancidity, and this characteristic suggests that products requiring a stable vegetable oil may create an important market opportunity. Possibilities include carriers for pesticides and plant hormones, water-evaporation retardants, products for sizing and waterproofing, and formulations for softening leather, paints, and adhesives.

The oil also has important potential as an additive to some plastics. It is crystallographically almost identical to, and miscible in all

Jojoba in Foods

When jojoba oil was administered in a single dose to rats, about 50 percent of it was absorbed, the rest being excreted in the feces. When jojoba oil was incorporated in the diets of rats at levels of 6 percent and 12 percent, its digestibility was about 40 percent. The rats showed a good tolerance to, and had no reluctance to eat, jojoba oil. At the 12-percent dietary level, they ate the same amount of food as the controls, but their body-weight gain was slightly lower and they were much leaner at the end: fat made up 7.6 percent of their body weight compared with 13 percent for the controls. At the 6-percent dietary level, they ate more food than the controls but maintained a comparable body weight.

The digested jojoba oil appears not to be accumulated in significant amounts in the body tissues. *In vitro* experiments show that the liver metabolizes it. One of the potential hazards of using jojoba oil in foods is that about 13 percent of its fatty acids are close to erucic acid in composition. Since this acid might contribute to heart disease, the hearts were examined histopathologically. Jojoba oil induced no lesions under the given experimental conditions.

A subchronic toxicity study was carried out to evaluate the safety of jojoba oil. The oil, fed to rats over a 2-month period, was incorporated into basal diet at 0.5, 5.0, and 10.0 percent (w/w) level. At weeks 4 and 13 of the experiment, transaminase and alkaline phosphatase levels increased in the plasma. This may indicate some liver damage, but no pathological lesions were found in the liver or other organs of the animals.

These results indicate that jojoba oil may have potential as an edible low-calorie oil for dieters, but before a wide application of jojoba oil in foods can be envisaged, safety aspects should be investigated further.

—Nestlé Products Technical Assistance
Orbe, Switzerland.

---

proportions with, low-density polyethylene. Hot jojoba oil readily dissolves polyethylene. The jojoba becomes microencapsulated and, over a period of days, diffuses out. This appears to be a fruitful area for research and product development.* Researchers have also suggested that jojoba oil should be examined as a potential polyethylene expander and as a lubricant for extrusion and molding.

---

* Information from T. Miwa.

Reacting jojoba oil with chlorine and bromine produces liquid derivatives that may be useful as solvents or as plasticizers for polymers. Of particular interest are bromo-derivatives, which may have fire-retardant characteristics.

Jojoba oil may also have promise in the treatment of wastewater and the recovery of rare metals. It has been used experimentally in Israel to recover radioactive metals from nuclear wastewater as well as to remove toxic heavy metals from industrial wastewater. Reportedly, it worked with high efficiency.*

Uses of Jojoba Wax

If it is priced competitively, jojoba wax appears to have commercial potential for substituting for several waxes that are now widely used. Hard waxes of this type are incorporated into floor finishes, carbon paper, coatings, masks, and sizings, as well as polishes for furniture, shoes, and automobiles. They are also employed to raise the melting point, gloss, and hardness of waxes used in paper, textiles, insulation, batteries, candles, matches, soaps, salves, crayons, and chalk. They are used to coat fruits and vegetables to retard shrinkage, reduce spoilage, minimize the effects of aging, and retain flavor. In the United States, some candy is also treated in this way so it doesn't melt in the hand. One hard wax, spermaceti, was once used by bakeries as a release agent and lubricant. Moreover, both spermaceti and beeswax have been used as carriers for medicines. Already, small amounts of jojoba wax are being purchased by U.S. cosmetics manufacturers as a substitute for Japan wax, a hard wax used especially in mascara.

Wax-in-water emulsions have been prepared from hydrogenated jojoba wax. The wax emulsified easily, and the prepared emulsion showed no sign of water separation—an indication of good stability—after more than one month.† This, combined with the excellent hardness of the hydrogenated product, should enhance its desirability in a variety of applications.

Hydrogenated jojoba oil buffs well and leaves a coat hard enough for use in both solvent- and emulsion-type floor waxes. One test, however, indicated that jojoba wax tends to crystallize out from an oil or solvent. To overcome this tendency, it can be blended with petroleum waxes to form gels that are unlikely to crystallize.

Jojoba wax has a high dielectric constant, an important property for use in insulators.

---

* Information from J. Wisniak.

† Information from T. Miwa. The emulsifying agents were 4 percent stearic acid and 2 percent triethanolamine, and the amount of wax was 30 percent in water.

TABLE 5 Hardness of Hydrogenated Jojoba Wax and Several Other Vegetable Waxes

Wax	Hardness[a]
Hydrogenated jojoba oil	1.9
Carnauba wax	2.6
Cane wax	2.1
Beeswax	0.38
Paraffin	0.24

[a] Brinel Hardness Number at 25°C, 4.3 kg load for 60 sec on 10.0 mm diameter steel ball.
SOURCE: T. K. Miwa

Household paraffin wax is hardened appreciably by the addition of jojoba wax. The paraffin's opalescent appearance changes to a creamy white, giving jojoba wax important potential markets in candlemaking. It is combustible, smokeless, and has a low ash content. It makes a brittle, unsatisfactory candle when used alone, but it blends well with other waxes to produce a high-quality product. The melting point is high enough that candles do not drip around the edges or melt during storage in warm climates.

Because of its crystallinity, jojoba wax appears unsatisfactory as a mold-release agent or as a plug for making molded objects; as the molten wax cools and solidifies it develops too many fracture lines. However, a small amount of additive (such as another wax) destroys the crystallinity and could be a way to overcome this limitation.

Partially hydrogenating jojoba oil, as previously noted, produces a range of soft white waxes whose properties are as yet unknown, but they may have good prospects in lipstick and cosmetics manufacture.

Jojoba Meal

The meal that remains after the oil has been extracted is a potentially valuable by-product. It could be of particular interest for feeding livestock because such feeds are often scarce in arid areas where the plant is grown. It contains about 30 percent protein as well as carbohydrate and fiber. Of the essential amino acids in its protein, the lysine content is good, but the methionine content is poor.

However, using jojoba meal in animal feeds is very uncertain at present because of an unusual toxic factor. The meal contains four compounds (collectively known as simmondsins) that animals find unpalatable. These are potentially hazardous because they contain cyano groups.

Of the different methods used to substantially decrease or eliminate simmondsins, fermentation using the bacterium of sweet (acidophilous) milk currently seems to be the most effective. The bacterium grows well on jojoba meal, and, after three weeks at room temperature, converts it to a palatable, nutritious feed. The resulting fermented meal is high in protein and is suitable for livestock, especially ruminants. In practice, the actual detoxification can be done by a process resembling the ensilage methods already used on many of the world's farms.*

Before jojoba meal can be accepted as a livestock feed, it must be shown that hazardous compounds cannot be transmitted to milk, meat, and eggs. In the United States, pertinent requirements of the Food and Drug Administration will have to be met.

---

* Information from A. Verbiscar.

6
Markets

Some rough guidelines to possible markets are given in this chapter. These are based mainly on precedents with other vegetable oils, and it should be emphasized once again that jojoba oil is unique, and when substantial quantities become available in consistent supply and at moderate prices, many new uses are likely to be discovered.

Jojoba oil remains stable during transport, and therefore, the world is its potential marketplace. Already, Japan is its largest user and has been importing a third of U.S. production in recent years, the equivalent of about 100 tons per year. In addition, West Germany and the Netherlands have together been importing a like amount.

Most of this has gone into specialty cosmetics. However, it seems clear that in the next 10 years far more oil than the cosmetics market can absorb will be produced. This means that jojoba marketers have to quickly develop new outlets. At first, these will probably be markets that already use other oils and waxes. For jojoba-based materials to penetrate such markets, they must be either cheaper or better than the present products. If there is no significant advantage in price or performance, manufacturers will refuse to bother with the expense and disruption of reformulating their products.

Sperm Oil Replacement

Sperm oil, obtained from the blubber and the head cavity of the sperm whale, has two main industrial uses: lubricant additives and leather-softening agents. Annual world production was approximately 150,000 tons in the mid 1960s and about 55,000 tons in 1977. It is even less today, not because of any inferiority in material, but because several countries have banned its importation. The United States, formerly the world's major consumer of sperm oil, prohibited its importation in 1971 as part of an endangered species conservation policy. Later, other countries adopted similar statutes.

Because of the growing shortage of sperm oil, various industries are looking for substitutes. Lubricant manufacturers are estimated to have satisfactorily replaced 80–90 percent of the sperm oil they originally used. The leather industry apparently has been unable to

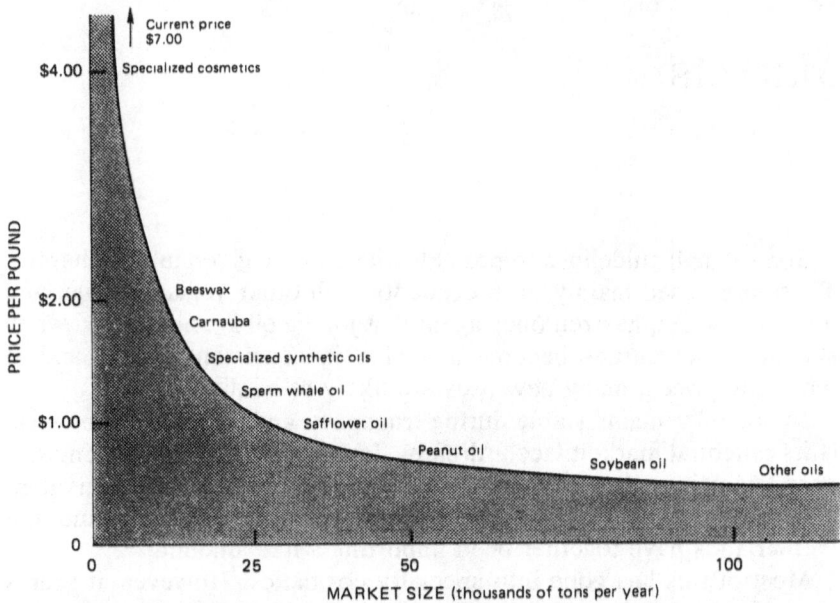

The future relationship between price and market size is unknown, but as prices fall, jojoba oil's potential markets will get much bigger.

find suitable replacements. Some synthetic oils have been developed for use in leather, but none appears to match the qualities of sulfonated sperm oil. Sulfonated jojoba oil should be a good replacement.

As long as jojoba oil is unavailable in quantity and at moderate prices, both the leather and lubricant industries are expected to continue with other substitutes.

At present, the remaining stocks of refined sperm oil are traded at prices up to $3,000 per ton. At such a price, the potential demand for jojoba oil, just for use in lubricants, has been estimated at 20,000–50,000 tons per year.*

Pharmaceuticals

The world market for pharmaceutical products is large. In 1979, it amounted to about $65 billion. In recent years, the real annual growth has increased at a rate of about 7 percent, and this pace is expected to continue, primarily because of the developing countries' ever-growing demand for pharmaceutical products.

Generally speaking, pharmaceuticals are expensive on a per-kilogram or per-ton basis. As a result, this sector is in a better position than

---

* Information from W. P. Miller.

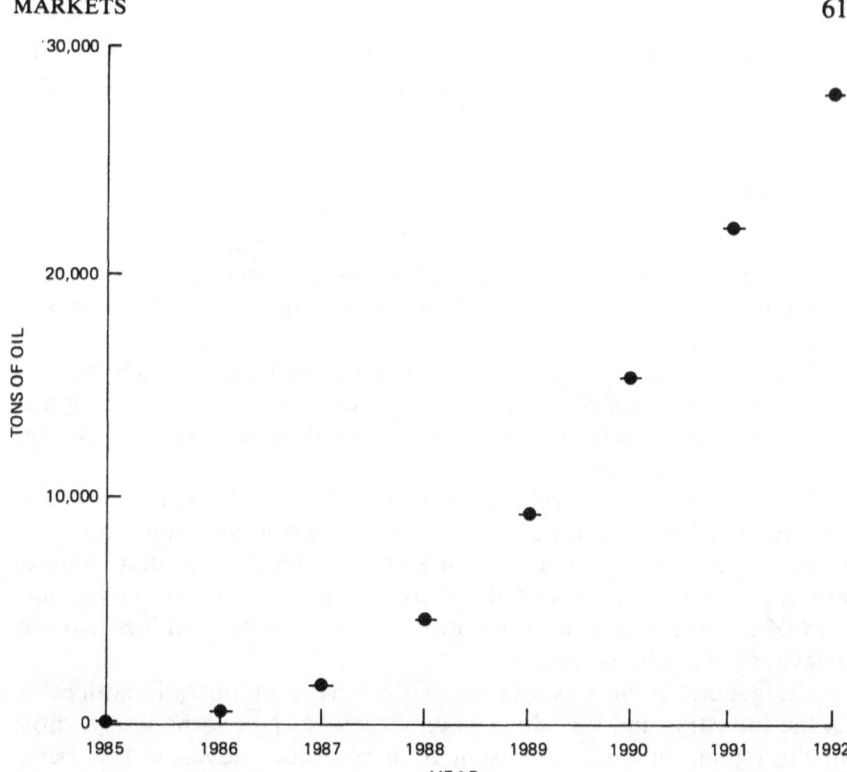

If the plantations already established live up to even modest expectations, the amount of jojoba oil available in future years will be substantial. This stylized graph shows one possible scenario. Floods, frosts, and other adversities can be expected to interrupt the smoothness of the curve. Unexpectedly low yields may shift the curve to the right so that the indicated yields are achieved in later years. Overall, however, the trend should be like that shown. The anticipated 1992 production is about the same as the amount of sperm oil that the United States was importing in the early 1970s. (Information from C. Whittaker)

any other to pay for low-production, high-quality ingredients such as today's jojoba oil, which is too costly for larger and cheaper markets.

As already mentioned, the oil's physical and chemical properties constitute a good basis for its prospective use as an antifoam agent in manufacture of antibiotics. As an indication of the size of this highly specialized market, the U.S. production of just one antibiotic, penicillin, in theory could absorb 8,000 tons (7 million kg) of jojoba oil annually. However, so far, the oil has been used only experimentally as an antifoam agent in penicillin production.

Although jojoba's potential for direct use in pharmaceuticals is currently being investigated (notably in formulations of ointments and creams for skin injuries and disorders), any newly developed products will have to pass public health tests before being introduced to the public. Clearly, it will take some years for jojoba oil to be used directly in pharmaceuticals on any significant scale.

Cosmetics

As mentioned previously, jojoba is already being used in various cosmetic products, but, in terms of world use, still on a small scale. Currently, it is largely small manufacturers that buy it for hair and skin preparations.

The greatly expanded use of jojoba oil in cosmetics seems to depend mainly on stable supplies and lower prices. It should increase significantly when supplies increase and prices drop as more plantations come into production.

The overall cosmetic industry has expanded steadily in recent years. The international trade in cosmetics increased at an annual real rate of about 13 percent between 1974 and 1978, reaching a total value of about $1.7 billion. Although the world market is relatively large, only part of it—hair and skin preparations, face makeup, and lipsticks—is relevant for jojoba oil and wax.

The general trend towards natural cosmetic products is noticeable in the industry, and this should benefit jojoba. Not surprisingly, most of the jojoba oil used at present is in cosmetics advertised as being "natural."

As its fundamental properties of stability and quality become more apparent, and its price drops with increasing production, jojoba oil could perhaps achieve sales to the cosmetics industry of between 10,000 and 12,000 tons per year.*

Waxes

If minor waxes such as spermaceti and ouricuri are included, the total international trade in animal and vegetable waxes is about 20,000 tons per year. The different types sell at average prices ranging between $3,000 and $6,500 per ton. This is expected to remain more or less stable, partly because of the increasing competition of synthetic waxes.

Once jojoba wax is available in commercial quantities on a regular basis, it may be able to seize a sizable part of the wax market, but only if it can be produced at prices comparable to those of waxes such as beeswax, carnauba, and candelilla. Some of the possibilities are described below.

---

* Information from W. P. Miller.

Beeswax Replacement. Most countries of the world produce their own beeswax, primarily by local beekeeping industries. The amount traded internationally is relatively static. Between 1972 and 1976, 5,000–5,500 tons were traded internationally each year. Ninety percent was absorbed by the United States, Japan, West Germany, the United Kingdom, France, the Netherlands, and Switzerland.

Beeswax is used in cosmetics (such as skin creams, emulsions, makeup foundations, face powders, rouge, hair creams, and lipsticks), food (candies), pharmaceuticals (ointments, coatings on pills), and candles.

Although quantities remained steady, prices for beeswax have risen over the years. Between 1973 and 1980, the international prices rose at an average annual rate of about 10 percent in real terms. Prices normally fluctuate in the range of $5,500 to $6,500 per ton.

On its technical merits, jojoba wax seems to be a suitable substitute for beeswax in many uses.

Carnauba Wax Replacement. Carnauba wax has many possible applications, but it is primarily used for carbon paper, floor polishes, car polishes, and cosmetics. Brazil is the only country that produces significant amounts. Its exports range from 10,000 to 14,000 tons annually. Prices range between $2,000 and $4,000 per ton, depending on quality. Jojoba wax seems a suitable replacement for carnauba in most applications. If its price drops to a point where it can compare with carnauba's, it is likely to capture some markets. This is primarily because carnauba is picked by hand and its prices are likely to rise quickly. Also, its supplies are under political control and could be subject to deliberate manipulation.

Candelilla Wax Replacement. Candelilla wax is used mainly in the manufacture of chewing gum, polishes, and cosmetics. Mexico, the only significant producer, increased its exports from about 2,000 tons in 1972 to about 2,500 tons in 1976. Prices ranged between $2,900 and $3,800 per ton, depending on quality.

Again, jojoba wax is a likely substitute. Its melting point is slightly higher and, because it is a cultivated rather than a wild plant, its supplies could be more stable and its prices more steady, thereby giving it the competitive edge.

The eventual possible demand for jojoba wax in all these uses is on the order of 5,000 to 10,000 tons per year, if its price is competitive.

7
Commercial Uncertainties

Potential investors contemplating farming jojoba should be cautious. Claims abound for the ease with which jojoba can be grown commercially, but jojoba requires a delay of about five years before it begins producing an income, and investing in the crop at this time appears to be suitable only for persons or organizations of substantial means. And investors should expect an economic risk for a long time.

Early jojoba growers, who rushed into planting without benefit of today's knowledge or experience to back up their management decisions, are likely to experience economic difficulties. Such situations occur with all farm crops; failure of imprudent ventures should not be viewed as an outright indictment of the long-term future of jojoba itself.

Actually, with almost any new crop comes failure and frustration, myths and misconceptions. (Avocados, kiwifruit, pecans, and pistachios all had turbulent beginnings in the United States, and yet all have become profitable, stable, national resources.) Patience and business acumen are essential. Interweaving plant science and business enterprise with market development is so complex that only a handful of farm crops have been successfully domesticated in modern times.

With potential industrial customers reluctant to estimate the quantity of jojoba oil they would consume, forecasts of market size must be based on tenuous assumptions of demand, supply, price, and any special technical benefits the oil might bring when compared with other oils. This means that, at present, there can be no foolproof projections of future price or demand.

Starting a Plantation

Jojoba is robust and adaptable, but it will not yield commercially significant amounts of oil just anywhere. It requires a congenial site: deep, well-drained soils, a hot, dry climate with little threat of frost, and preferably a reliable supply of water. Farmers should look for frost-free, low-lying, semiarid land. It should be fairly level if irrigated farming is to be practiced.

COMMERCIAL UNCERTAINTIES

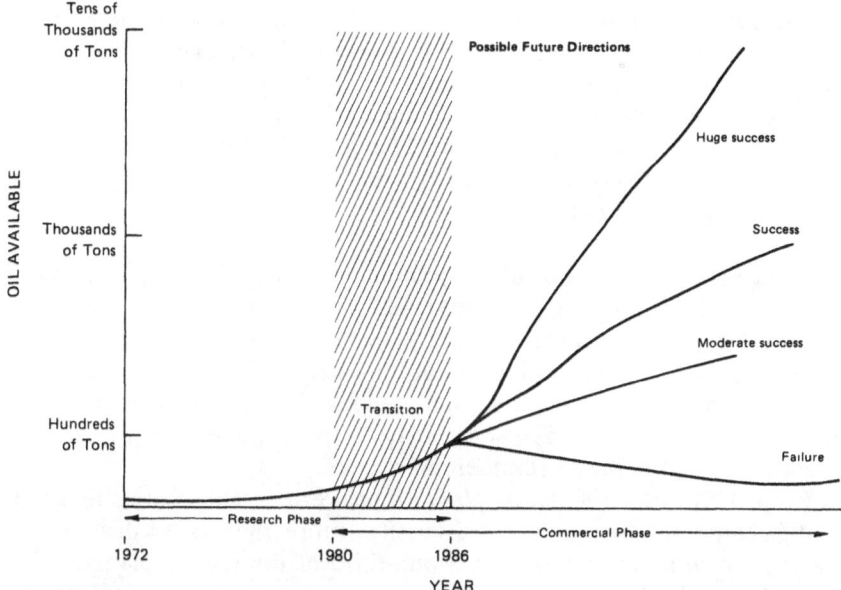

Jojoba development. Jojoba is now at a crossroads and its future course of development is uncertain. Its commercial testing time is still ahead.

Temperature. Before proceeding, growers should carefully investigate the area's climatic history to make sure the temperature rarely falls below 23°F (−5°C) for extended periods. With a permanent crop like this, a single severe frost every 10 years could doom a commercial endeavor or require expensive frost-protection devices. Mature plants can survive a medium frost (such as 25°F), but it kills their flower buds so that no crop results that growing season.

To judge a site's suitability, local weather data detailing lowest temperatures in previous decades should, if possible, be obtained. Even this may not be enough to determine specific local conditions because variations can occur within a few miles of where the data were recorded. Rolling terrain is especially tricky because on frosty nights pockets of cold air can form in low sites.

Rainfall. Although native stands of jojoba grow where rainfall can drop to as low as 4 inches (100 mm) a year, the plant needs more than that for profitable production in commercial plantations. A mature plantation, for example, probably needs at least 18-22 inches (460–560 mm) of water a year to be commercially viable, at least in industrialized countries.

Sex Determination. At present, it is not possible to determine whether a seedling is male or female until it flowers. This makes it difficult to position the male plants in a plantation. The problem can be circumvented by planting and then "roguing out" the unwanted males (and inferior females) once they bloom. Using cuttings or tissue culture to vegetatively propagate plants of a known sex allows the grower to avoid this problem entirely.

Plant Selection. Genetically, jojoba is extremely diverse. It displays variations in branching patterns, leaf size, earliness of flowering, number of fruits per node, fruiting pattern, and male to female ratios. This diversity results in large variations between individual plants in the time they take to mature, their seed yield, and their adaptability to a given site. This adds enormously to the complexities the grower must master to achieve commercial success.

From 1978 until 1983 most plantations were established using seed, and because of their inherent diversity, more than two-thirds of the yield may come from fewer than one-third of the female plants.

Such variability, however, also provides opportunities to select and breed for optimal characteristics. It is vital to find and replicate quality specimens—planting them will result in plantations that yield more rapidly and several times higher than has been possible heretofore.

Management

It is a widespread myth that jojoba needs no management. Like other crops, it requires skill and care to ensure a financial return. Weed control and fertilization, for example, can significantly influence yield and profitability. Of five 4-year-old Israeli plots using identical seed but different management techniques, one produced 1,350 kg of seed per hectare, another 1,050 kg per hectare, and three averaged only 162 kg per hectare.

There is also a misconception that jojoba doesn't need irrigation. That assertion may be true for survival, but, in most cases, not for maximum production.

Yields

Because the crop is so new, definite projections cannot be made about yields of fully mature plantations. One factor complicating yield projections is the consistency of bearing. Jojoba is not inherently an alternate-bearing crop, but some plants do bear prolifically one year and bear almost nothing the next; others are much more consistent.

COMMERCIAL UNCERTAINTIES

The reasons for this need to be clarified, and ways to overcome inconsistency translated into management practices.

Plantation spacing is another complication in yield projections. Although a density of 900–1,000 female plants per acre (2,200–2,500 per hectare) seems to be a good target, some growers aim for twice that many, preferring to remove the less desirable plants later as they become identifiable. (This is an uncertain process because the low, early yielders may be the high bearers in the long run. And the bushes can get so intertwined that removing one without damaging another is almost impossible.) Other growers aim for only 500 plants per acre (1,240 per hectare) and may interplant other crops between the young bushes to provide income during the early years.

By and large, researchers don't agree on likely yields in commercial plantations. Three of their different projections are listed below:

- *Conservative*. University of Arizona researchers project yields of 0.5 pounds (200 g) of seed per plant (without roguing or selection) at age 5 years, and 1 pound (0.5 kg) of seed per plant at age 10. This is based on the average yield of the various plants in their germplasm collection at Mesa, Arizona.

- *Moderate*. University of California researchers believe that 3–4 pounds (1.3–1.8 kg) of seed from seedling-derived plants 7–8 years old is within reach. And they believe that by planting cuttings taken from the best plants available, 4–5 pounds (1.8–2.3 kg) of seed per plant seems realistic.

- *Optimistic*. In a university experimental plot in California, some trees have yielded 7 pounds (2.6 kg) per plant each year from their eighth year onward. Although this provides hope for especially good yields in the future, it is generally observed that yields in farm fields are not as abundant as those in university experimental plots.

At present, a yield of 200 pounds per acre (200 kg per hectare) from 4- to 5-year-old shrubs and of 3,000 pounds of seed per acre (3,000 kg per hectare) from an 11- to 12-year-old plantation appears to be a realistic expectation from well-managed, carefully selected plants. But no plantations are yet old enough to actually produce this amount—the average yield worldwide is 0.7 pounds (300 g) per plant in the fourth year.

As better plants are selected and vegetatively propagated, dramatic increases in yield and decreases in maturing time will occur. Already, in Israel, 3.5-year-old superior plants, propagated by tissue culture, have yielded an average of 3 pounds (1.2 kg) per plant. (The high was 1.5 kg and the low was 0.4 kg per plant.) Also in Israel, a 2-hectare plot near Mohav yielded 3.3 pounds (1.5 kg) per plant in the fourth year.

Processing

The existing jojoba-processing facilities in the United States have a capacity to produce 1.6 million pounds (0.7 million kg) of oil per year, but they actually run at only about 20 percent capacity because of the limited amount of seed available from the native crop and from the young plantations. These factories, running at a fraction of their actual capacity, extract the oil at a price of 50–75 cents per pound of oil ($1.10–$1.65 per kg). This high cost currently adds a commercial uncertainty, but, at maximum production (which should be achieved in the next few years), these facilities should be able to routinely extract the oil at a cost of 8–12 cents per pound (18–26 cents per kg).*

Plantings Outside North America

With a crop so new, commercial viability outside the plant's native habitat still needs to be proved. Trial plots are encouraged, but, for the time being, massive plantings of jojoba outside the Sonoran Desert are not recommended. Although there is little doubt that jojoba will survive in Africa and the Middle East and other similar climates, there is as yet no certainty that the crop will set enough seed to be commercially profitable.

Competing Substances

Orange Roughy Oil. The orange roughy, a fish recently discovered in the deep waters off the coast of New Zealand, produces an oil of the wax-ester type. Fillets of this fish have become a popular delicacy in New Zealand and increasingly in Japan and North America.

Orange roughy oil is being commercially extracted from the waste material left after filleting the meat.† Made up predominantly of C-36, C-38, and C-40 wax esters, it is contaminated with up to 5 percent triglycerides, as well as saturated and unsaturated fatty acids and fatty alcohols ranging from C-14 to C-24. Perhaps because of the free acids, the raw oil is unusually corrosive, causing rubber and polymeric seals to decay; this has delayed its introduction into commerce.

Reportedly, an estimated 2,500 tons of orange roughy oil could be produced annually from the catch allocated by the New Zealand government's fishing laws. By comparison, the amount of jojoba now

---

* Information from C. Whittaker
† Fish oils extracted from two other South Pacific deepwater species, the black oreo and the small-spined oreo, also contain this type of oil.

in cultivation today should produce 10 times that amount when the plantations reach maturity.

Jojoba oil is generally of longer chain length than this fish oil, it has no triglycerides, and requires no deodorization or "preservation" prior to use.

"Synthetic Jojoba." During the past two years, as jojoba oil prices rose because of increased demand and a poor harvest from the native crop, several chemical companies have produced "jojoba substitutes." One company in West Germany already makes a jojoba-like liquid wax out of high-erucic rapeseed oil and sells about two tons of it a week. Some physical characteristics (such as color and odor, infrared absorption patterns, and viscosities) of these so-called jojoba substitutes are similar to those of pure jojoba oil, but little information has yet been published that compares their range of functional properties with those of jojoba oil itself.

In experiments, jojoba substitutes have been made from the oils of plants such as crambe, limnanthus (meadowfoam), lunaria, and rapeseed. Like other vegetable oils, these are triglyceride oils, but their fatty acids have about the same carbon chain length as those in jojoba. To transform them into the substitute takes three chemical transformations: the oils are hydrolyzed and their fatty acids chemically separated from the glycerol, half the fatty acids are reduced to alcohols, and the resulting alcohols are esterified with the remaining half of the acids to form the wax ester.

Such a process currently produces a cheaper product than jojoba oil. But when the full jojoba crop comes on stream, it seems likely that the cost advantage will be reversed.

Compared with these competitors, jojoba has two major technical advantages: high natural purity and a single double bond in each of its acid and alcohol portions. Most other vegetable oils have a greater amount of unsaturation, and when chemically transformed into derivatives (for lubricants, factices, and other industrial products), the extra double bonds lead to tars and gums that are detrimental in many uses.

Biotechnology. Plant scientists have found that tissue from immature jojoba seeds (2 months after pollination) can be artificially cultured. As the cells of these "test-tube embryos" multiply, they produce an oil identical to that in jojoba seeds. It is thought that such tissues might be cultured en masse, thus bypassing the plant and generating jojoba oil in a factory. At present, though, this process cannot compete economically with jojoba oil flowing from plantations.

In future it may be possible to put jojoba genes in bacteria and produce jojoba oil by fermentation. This possibility also seems far distant because five or six genes are involved in producing the oil, and it would take a lifetime of painstaking research to get them transferred and activated in a microorganism.*

---

* Information from C. W. Lee.

8
Jojoba Industry Needs

Despite the fact that growers have developed suitable farming practices, the industry is only now beginning to achieve the credibility, cohesiveness, and efficiency required for large-scale commercial success.

Indeed, jojoba has had to overcome a dubious reputation: a few promoters made outrageous claims (especially in deals associated with land speculation); others sold oil of questionable quality; and some manufactured products claiming to contain jojoba that in fact contained none. The enormous price increases in 1981 and 1982 (when the wild crop was sparse and prices rose to $10,000 a barrel) disenchanted many potential long-term customers. Further, the lack of standards and quality control has not helped jojoba's image with its most important audience, the manufacturers of consumer products.

Because of irregularities in the weather, the supply of jojoba oil to the market is still erratic and unreliable. (In parts of Arizona the 1984 crop was lost to a "freak" flood, the 1985 crop to frost.) As a result, potential purchasers have had no assurance of a consistent supply of dependable quality oil at a stable price. Consequently, major industrial corporations are not using jojoba in their products as yet.

Market Development

The jojoba industry can only realize its profit potential if it now applies the same effort to market development as it applied to propagation and farming practices. The major challenge is to increase the number of companies that utilize jojoba in their products.

Potential users have already shown reluctance to incorporate jojoba into their products because they lack technical information, have only limited experience in handling it, and suffer from a dearth of cost-benefit data—all of which has been compounded by the absence of an assured supply.

Growers and processors must now concentrate on helping industry develop and market jojoba products by educating buyers and technical personnel. For example, they must help substantiate the claims made for jojoba oil and its many uses.

The manufacturer, on the other hand, has an opportunity to create a new, national, renewable resource by cooperating with the jojoba industry in developing products that utilize jojoba oil at prices that match the requirements of today's producers.

Pricing

Some of the problems growers face in achieving an adequate return follow.*

- *Today*. During these early years—when production is low, harvesting costs high, and plantation development costs are being borne—a U.S. grower needs to receive about $2.00 per pound ($4.40 per kg) for his seed to break even.† Producing 1 pound of oil takes up to 2.5 pounds (1.1 kg) of seed, and extracting it in low volume costs 50¢ per pound ($1.10 per kg) of oil. This means that the selling price for oil from today's plantations has to be about $5.50 per pound, the equivalent of $40.00 per gallon, ($12.00 per kg; $8.80 per liter).

- *The near future*. In higher volumes, processing is more cost-efficient (especially with solvent extraction) and can be done at 8¢ per pound (18¢ per kg). Therefore, as supplies increase, the price of oil should soon drop to $4.00 per pound, or $30.00 per gallon ($9.00 per kg; $6.60 per liter). This will still give the grower a selling price of $2.00 per pound ($4.40 per kg) of seed.

- *Long term*. With increasing production, improved harvesting, and a yield of 2,000 pounds (910 kg) of oil per acre, the break-even cost should come down to $2.00 per pound of oil, the equivalent of $15.00 per gallon ($4.40 per kg; $3.30 per liter). This situation is within reach as the latest clones are planted.

Eventually, jojoba oil must be competitively priced with the products it is replacing. To reach the mass markets for lubricants and hard waxes, it must be priced below $2.00 a pound ($4.40 per kg). At that level, the demand would far exceed supply, and plantings would have to increase substantially all over the world just to keep up.‡

---

* This section deals with jojoba pricing in the United States. Information supplied by C. Whittaker.

† The break-even costs are high because the grower has 5 or 6 years of expenses with no income. After about year 8, when the cost of establishing the plantation has been amortized, break-even costs could be much lower.

‡ Preliminary results from the sparse information available indicate that jojoba oil outperforms its competitors and at a lower additive level. Thus, it may well be that jojoba oil at, say, $5.00 per pound ($11.00 per kg) is more cost-effective than a synthetic lubricant additive at $2.00 per pound ($4.40 per kg). But this is not proven.

A long-term target sale price is close to 50¢ per pound of plantation seed ($1.10 per kg), which is equivalent to an oil price about $8.00 per U.S. gallon ($1.80 per liter). This general level seems realistic in the future world marketplace. It represents a gross output of $1,000 per acre at a ton of seed per acre ($2,470 per hectare at 2.47 tons of seed per hectare).

Reducing Production Costs

Efficient plantation management is the key to the future of the jojoba industry. Commercial growers must concentrate on vigorous cost control—slashing to the minimum production costs per acre, per bush, and per pound.

9
Research Needs

Basic research, the underpinning for the crop's future development, deserves greater support. Government agencies, foundations, corporations, and individuals who fund agricultural research should support jojoba studies. Some particular needs are listed below.

Agronomic Research

Agricultural Practices

Jojoba has demonstrated a favorable response to many of the practices and techniques currently used in agriculture, but research is needed to understand its unique properties that can be manipulated to coax the crop to reach its fullest potential. Among agronomic questions that cannot be readily answered with assurance are:

- What plant spacing is best?
- What ratio of females to males is best?
- When is the best time to irrigate, and how much should be applied?
- What is the best method to control weeds?
- What are jojoba's fertilization requirements?
- When is the best time to prune? How little, how much, and what part of the plant to prune?
- What criterion should be the basis for selecting superior plants?
- What is the best way to harvest: By hand? By machine? And what type of harvester: Over-the-row? Vacuum?
- What is the relationship between a superior plant at a young age and long-term performance?

All these questions point to valuable areas for research and testing.

Plant Selection

It is vital to find and replicate quality jojoba specimens. They will produce plantations that yield faster and several times higher than has

RESEARCH NEEDS 75

been possible heretofore. In making selections among different jojoba plants, the most significant yield components to consider are:

- Seed production at every node;
- Large seed size;
- High oil content in the seed;
- Late flowering (to escape frost damage);
- Precocity (for instance, starting seed production before the third year);
- Consistent production from year to year; and
- Upright growth habit (for easy harvesting).

To combine all these features in one superior variety will require years of persistent selection and testing. The recent availability of vegetative propagation, however, makes possible its more rapid accomplishment. It is desirable to measure the average annual yield of oil over as many years as possible before massively propagating any clone.

Some particular points of plant selection follow.

Reducing Plant Size. At present, the optimal biomass for maximum seed production is unknown. However, vegetative growth should be reduced as much as possible without severely reducing seed production. Dwarf varieties have less nutritional demand, they allow more plants to be grown per acre, and they can make harvesting easier.

Synchronizing Flowering. Many generations of breeding have gone into making conventional crops flower uniformly. All wheat plants, for example, flower within a few days of each other in many environments. Because most jojoba plantations have been established using heterogeneous seed, flowering is not synchronized. To get seeds maturing at the same time would be an important benefit to a grower. Research should focus on genetic traits as well as on management techniques. The goal should be to develop high-yielding clones that ripen uniformly and can be harvested in one pass.

Selecting Superior Males. So far, there has been little selection of male plants. Current types are variable: some have short flowering seasons, others long. To select male plants that produce an abundance of flowers, shed pollen over a long period, and result in superior seeds (with high oil content, for example) is a particular research need. In selecting superior males, some criteria to look for are: large clusters of flowers; tallness (so that the pollen disseminates well), plants whose pollen has long viability, and plants that produce pollen at the time when females are receptive.

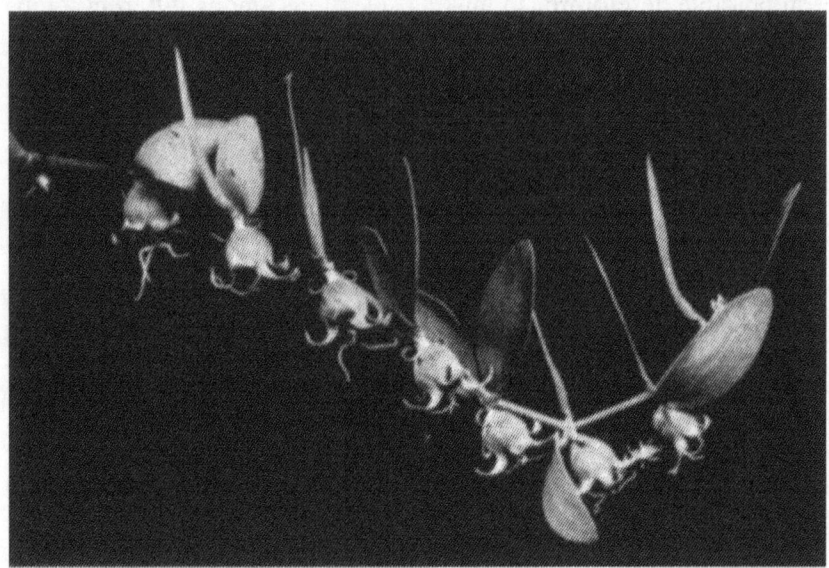

Uniform flowering on a bush in New South Wales, Australia. A target for growers and researchers should be to produce fields in which the flowers all open at the same time. At present, flowering is variable and multiple harvests must be made to collect the seeds, because they ripen at different times. (R. L. Dunstone and I. A. Dawson)

Increasing Oil Content. It is important to select plants with a high percentage of oil in the seeds. The average oil content is 50 percent—a substantial figure—but seeds with 63 percent oil have been discovered. A diligent improvement project (which would be facilitated by a simple method for testing oil content) could almost certainly boost the oil content of the plantation seeds by 20 percent. This is important because the target for all growers, after all, should be not the seed yield per acre, but the oil yield per acre.

Harvesting

The question of how to harvest jojoba mechanically is a pressing one. This is not strictly an engineering challenge: the harvest's outcome depends on the plant and machine fitting together. A clone that may yield exceptionally may be prohibitively expensive to harvest. For example, some have short internodes and are tight bushes, and a mechanized picker requires a somewhat open bush that its "fingers" can comb through. (The density of the bush is less important if the seed is to be swept or sucked off the ground.)

Features that fit a plant to harvesting by picker are:

- Upright growth with a clear base for access;
- Maximal density for high yields, but not too dense for efficient picking;
- Uniform timing of female flower receptivity;
- Annually consistent female receptivity;
- Uniform maturity of seeds on each selected plant;
- Optimal fruit removal (requires assessment of natural dehiscence and the force needed to shake seeds off);
- Flexible limbs that are not easily damaged by harvesters; and
- Minimal root and stem suckering (to keep open access to the base of the plants).

Combating Desertification

Claims have been made that jojoba has potential for overcoming "desert creep." This possibility deserves to be explored. In its favor, jojoba has a hardy, drought-tolerant nature. More importantly, it produces a high-value product in drylands, thus giving inhabitants an incentive to stay "on the farm" and protect their land from the advancing desert creep by growing other species that may halt the threatening sand dunes.

Product Research

Jojoba offers many areas for chemists and industrial researchers to explore. As noted previously, the oil has been transformed into at least 50 derivatives that seem to have commercial utility. This wealth of new compounds deserves careful evaluation and development.*

A few broad research subjects are highlighted here.

Lubricants

Qualification Testing. Jojoba oil has performed exceedingly well in small-scale diagnostic lubricant tests. It has not yet, however, been assessed in documented, full-scale trials conducted in actual operating equipment and compared against controls. This is a vital need.

Full qualification trials will take several years because the steps include formulating blends for different purposes, putting them into operating engines, and measuring performance features such as engine

---

* Indeed, the whole topic of wax esters, whether they be from jojoba, from fish oils, or from synthesized materials, deserves much greater recognition from chemists. Useful first steps would be a comprehensive review paper, a symposium, or a book devoted to wax esters.

output, heat build-up, oil stability, and performance life.* The cost for such an evaluation would be high: perhaps $250,000 for formulating and bench-testing blends, and perhaps $500,000 for in-service testing. But until this is done, uncertainty over jojoba oil's potential in the lubrication industry will remain. And without published evaluations that are accepted by the automotive industry, the oil cannot penetrate broad markets.†

Overcoming the High Pour Point. The fact that jojoba oil tends to solidify in cool weather is a particular problem if it is to be used as a base stock in the automotive industry in temperate-zone countries. Therefore, a particular research need is to find uses in which this is not a concern, or to lower the point at which the oil thickens. This latter might be tackled from the plant end—there are indications, for example, that growing jojoba in hot regions produces oil of lower molecular weight. It might also be tackled from the chemical end— jojoba oil can be trans-esterified with different acids and alcohols to produce many shorter chain esters with widely different freezing points and viscosities.

The high pour point is a problem mainly if the oil is to be used as a base stock. If used as an additive, it is unlikely to be a serious concern.

Derivatives as Lubricants. The straight oil has excellent metal-wetting properties and gives metal a slippery surface. The sulfurized oil is valuable at high temperatures and pressures, which create metal-sulfur links that chemically bond the jojoba molecule to the metal surface. But other derivatives with good lubricating qualities are also likely to be found. Adding dimercaptothiadiazole to the jojoba molecule, for instance, reduces the (already extremely good) coefficient of friction by 20 percent, and the product protects copper against corrosion at the same time.‡

Cutting Oils. Jojoba oil might find a particular niche in cutting fluids that are used to cool, lubricate, prevent rust, and flush away chips in metal-working machines. Because these emulsions are aqueous and are continuously recycled, they grow bacteria and fungi, and because they get on workers' hands, even slightly toxic preservatives cannot be added. Jojoba, because it is largely resistant to microbial attack, may be of particular benefit in this application.

---

* A paper identifying the requirements for completely evaluating jojoba oil as a lubricant is available from R. M. Estefan, Southwest Research Institute, 6220 Culebra Road, San Antonio, Texas 78284, USA.
† For example, in most cases the vehicle manufacturer's approval will be required if the vehicle's warranty is not to be voided.
‡ Information from P. Landis.

Jet Engine Lubricants. Its high-temperature stability and excellent viscosity index suggest the possibility of jojoba oil's use as an additive in jet engine lubricants. To assess this is an important research need. Its thermal and oxidative stability, as well as its decomposition products, would have to be analyzed.

Magnetic Memory Media Lubricants. The stable ester structure of jojoba oil might make it suitable as a lubricant for reducing frictional wear in floppy discs, digital tape, audio tape, magnetizable film, and other magnetic memory media.

Sperm oil is (or has been) widely used as an internal lubricant in audio and video recording tapes to reduce wear on the tape itself and on the recording/playback heads. With the demise of sperm oil, this is another use for which jojoba should be tested.

High-Temperature Oils

Jojoba oil's viscosity index is almost twice that of most petroleum oils. Although there is some disagreement over the actual number, it is in the range of 190 to 230, whereas the mineral oils are in the range of 90 to 100. Viscosity index is a measure of a liquid's change in viscosity with changing temperature. As they get hot, liquids with lower indexes get thinner than those with higher indexes. Normally an increase in viscosity index of just two or three points means a big improvement in the lubricating quality of an oil as it heats up. Jojoba oil with a viscosity index 100 points higher than average could boost low-grade oils even in small amounts. This possibility should excite the interest of all industries that want an oil to maintain its viscosity as it is heated.

Fermentations

Scores of widely used fermentations suffer from excessive foaming. Sperm oil was once commonly used to overcome this problem, but in its absence silicone oil or vegetable oils are used. Jojoba oil deserves investigation because it seems to have particular advantages over these. Unlike silicone oil it is biodegradable and should not build up a gummy layer inside the fermentation vessels and pipes. On the other hand, it is less biodegradable than conventional vegetable oils and is probably largely inert to most of the fermentation organisms. Thus it could be more effective than the triglyceride oils. Fermentations producing antibiotics, steroids, alcohol, and citric acid are some in which jojoba oil deserves testing as an antifoam.

Medicinal Effects

Possible Anti-Inflammatory Effects. Preliminary indications suggest that jojoba oil has beneficial effects on acute and chronic inflammation of the skin. The possibility that jojoba oil could be beneficial in the treatment of sunburn and perhaps more serious burns should be investigated.

The oil is absorbed into skin through secondary structures such as hair follicles (see picture page 51). Further research is needed into this percutaneous absorption, and particularly its effects on the inflammatory response. The research could involve *in-vitro* assays to look at the effects on neutrophils and the blastic response, as well as *in-vivo* assays on animals and humans.

Possible Antimicrobial Effects. Jojoba oil has shown antimicrobial effects *in-vitro,* and research to investigate its ability to counteract acute and chronic skin and other infections is warranted.

A particularly interesting research area is to test jojoba oil's effects on tuberculosis, leprosy, and brucellosis. The bacteria causing these diseases shelter inside "cocoons" of wax and are difficult to reach with antibiotics. (The current treatment for TB, for instance, requires that patients take medication each day for a year or more.) The waxes are made up of esters whose chemical structure is like that of jojoba oil, although their chain lengths are much longer. Because of the chemical similarity, it seems possible that the liquid jojoba oil could help dissolve the solid wax coatings around the bacilli. An antibiotic used with jojoba as a "penetrating oil" might be a particularly effective combination. This suggestion is highly speculative, but in view of the widespread nature of these diseases, and their relative resistance to attack, the possibility deserves at least preliminary assessment.

Food

The idea of using jojoba oil as a low-calorie oil for human consumption is tantalizing. Potentially, it is the largest market of all for jojoba. Both the oil and the roasted seeds have long been eaten by Indians in the Sonoran Desert region, but extensive trials are necessary before jojoba can be approved for use as a modern foodstuff for sale to the general public.

So far, experiments in rats have shown no fundamental barriers to the concept of using jojoba oil as a foodstuff, but much more basic research is needed before the Food and Drug Administration or its equivalent overseas will authorize its use. This research should be carried out, but to complete it will take at least two-and-a-half years of concentrated research and an expenditure of an estimated $2.5 million, and there is no guarantee that some health hazard won't be uncovered.

Appendix A
Jojoba Outside North America

Today, the largest jojoba plantations are in the United States, but more and more countries are establishing trial plots or growing the crop commercially. Sizable plantations are under cultivation in Australia, Brazil, Costa Rica, Israel, Mexico, South Africa, and a few other nations. Experimental plots exist in several dozen more. Below is a rough overview of those that have been most widely reported. This is no more than a passing snapshot of the scene in 1984–1985; with so much planting going on, as well as the natural failures of some trials, no single statement can remain current for long.

These experiences, however small, are significant beyond their size. From such early plantings, nations can get an inkling of how well the crop may fare within their borders. Potential investors can observe the variability inherent in jojoba propagated by seed. And growers are likely to discover high-yielding plants with particular adaptability to local conditions. Thus, plantings like these could be the nucleus for a "second generation" of superior plants. If vegetatively propagated, quality specimens of this kind will much increase the likelihood of bringing successful jojoba farming to the region.

Indeed, any area proposing to begin jojoba production should establish seeded plots for observation, monitoring, and germplasm selection. In most cases, these will not produce profitable amounts of oil for large-scale commerce, but they are a vital foundation for building a flourishing jojoba-growing industry.

Latin America

Mexico

Extensive harvesting of the native jojoba stands of Baja California and the state of Sonora in northwestern Mexico began in the 1970s. The large quantities of seed gathered from these wild shrubs has made Mexico the world's principal producer of jojoba oil. Jojoba oil extraction companies have been established at Hermosillo, Ensenada, Caborca, and other centers. Most of the product is exported to Japan, but five different brands of jojoba cosmetics are marketed in Mexico.

After 12 years of research on cultivation, harvesting, extraction, and commercialization of seed and oil, Mexico has been able to establish the foundation of a jojoba-based industry. About 2,500 acres (1,000 hectares) of private jojoba farms have become the early proving grounds for the crop. In most areas of northwestern Mexico, the plants are growing well in both dry-farmed and irrigated areas.

Near Hermosillo, the captial of Sonora, some 3.5-year-old plants are 5–6 feet (1.5–2 m) tall and are bearing 50–80 pounds of seed per acre (60–80 kg per hectare). Reportedly, they have required neither pesticides nor fertilization, and some have not been irrigated (after initial establishment), although rainfall in the area is only 8 inches (200 mm) and summer temperatures reach 120°F (49°C).

Costa Rica

Several commercial plantations have been started in Costa Rica. The first sites selected were in the central highlands, where both soils and climate seem unlikely for good jojoba production. However, after some setbacks the plants are now reported to be growing satisfactorily. Newer plantings in the arid lowlands of Guanacaste province are showing good growth and set seed for the first time in 1984.

Curaçao

A few plants are reportedly thriving and bearing well on this arid Caribbean island.

Peru

An experimental plantation has been installed in an arid area near Ica.

Chile

To foster reforestation, the Chilean government provides substantial financial benefits to tree planters; it also has huge amounts of bare, dry land where rainfall is insufficient for conventional crops. This has stimulated considerable experimentation with jojoba.

Investigations were initiated in 1977 through the National Institute of Agricultural Investigations (INIA), the National Forestry Corporation (CONAF), the University of Chile, The Corporación de Fomento de la Producción (CORFO—which has 15 hectares or 37 acres in 12 different locations), Fundación Chile, and several private organizations. The Forestry Department has planted experimental plots as well.

APPENDIX A: JOJOBA OUTSIDE NORTH AMERICA 83

Beyond these experiments and trials, there are 300 acres (120 hectares) of commercial plantations. The oldest is five years old and is in the Camarones Valley in the arid north (latitude 19°S.), where the plant is growing well.

Argentina

The climate of northwestern Argentina is similar to that of the Sonoran Desert. Experimental plantings of jojoba were first carried out in 1977 and 1978 at Villa Dolores in the province of Cordoba. Subsequent plantings were made in the province of Mendoza and, in 1981, in the province of Tucuman.

At Villa Dolores some impressively productive plants, with dense clusters of seeds, have been discovered. Some 6-year-old plants are each producing 0.8 pounds (350 g) of clean, dry seed per year. Most plots are unirrigated, and the region gets an annual rainfall of 14 inches (350 mm).

A major plantation is being established near Cartamarca.

Paraguay

Trial plantations are being conducted in Paraguay's Chaco Desert region. One small experimental plot is 6 years old, and the plants are surviving despite receiving no care. Some other plots have 2-year-old plants that are 2 feet (60 cm) high and are setting flowers and seeds, which is faster than in the United States. In 1985, growers are planting 3,200 acres (1,300 hectares) of commercial plantations.

All in all, Paraguayans are hopeful that jojoba can be established as a common crop for the dry Chaco region where little else can be successfully grown.

Brazil

For the arid northeast of Brazil, jojoba is a promising crop. Since 1976, it has performed well in test plots near Fortaleza, Ceara (latitude 4°S). The first experimental plot was sown on the Campus do Pici, of the Federal University of Ceara in Fortaleza. Between 1977 and 1980, additional small plots were installed in surrounding areas. There are now about 250 acres (100 hectares) of experimental sites throughout Ceara State.

In Fortaleza, some 6- and 7-year-old plants, grown with no irrigation, have reached heights of almost 10 feet (3 m). Some are producing seed in the third year. However, the area's high humidity causes outbreaks of fungal disease in the rainy season.

Erkowit, Sudan. Healthy, strong jojoba bearing seed at age three years. The fact that the crop can produce in a region so unlike its native habitat gives hope that the crop can be a global resource. (N. D. Vietmeyer)

This work was pioneered by the Federal University of Ceara, but corporations and private individuals are now getting involved. In 1982 about 3,000 acres (1,200 hectares) of commercial plantations were established—some unirrigated, and many interplanted with cowpea, cassava, and cotton in the rainy season.

In the northern part of the state of Minas Gerais and the southern part of Bahia, a private company has recently initiated plantations covering more than 2,500 acres (1,000 hectares).

Africa

Sudan

Sudan has become a leader in introducing jojoba to Africa. Test plots are scattered across the arid northern half of the country, some of them sites with furnacelike heat, desiccating winds, blowing sand, and almost no rainfall. Jojoba has survived all these adversities, although most of the plants have received at least modest irrigation. The areas vary from 3 to 5 acres (1.2–2 hectares) and are located at Dongola, Erkowit, Hudeida, El Rawakeeb, Bara, and Sag el Naam.

This successful establishment is encouraging, especially as the latitude (about 17°N) is so different from that of the plant's native habitat. But survival is not enough: it is jojoba *seed* that is the commercial goal, and the plants have formed seed at only two locations as yet, notably at Erkowit, a barren upland area not far from the Red Sea.

Although the production has so far been limited, Sudan's early success in obtaining seed from the crop indicates that jojoba might have a significant commercial future elsewhere in the Middle East and the Sahelian zone of Africa.

Kenya

Jojoba was first planted in Kenya in 1977, and today, small trial plantings are scattered in various research stations. For example, some seedlings are growing well near Lake Turkana. A private farm near Voi has 100 acres (40 hectares) planted with seed from California.

Tanzania

Small trial plantations near Moshe and Dodoma have shown that the plant can survive in Tanzania.

Zimbabwe

In 1980, the Horticultural Investigation Centre of Zimbabwe established nine experimental plots in areas of differing climate and soil, but mainly concentrated in areas with rainfall under 24 inches (600 mm) per year.

Although commercial plantings have not yet been undertaken, some of the plants in the southern part of the country—in the low veld—look promising enough for economic production.

Botswana

There is some interest in jojoba in Botswana, especially for tribal and communal lands, but so far, few plants have actually been grown. Vast areas of the country appear suitable for the crop, but trials are necessary to judge the plant's adaptability more accurately.

South Africa

In the late 1970s, the South African Department of Agriculture and Fisheries sent seeds to experiment stations in various parts of the country. Also, trial batches of seed were sent by private enthusiasts to farms all over South Africa. Those planted at Oudtshoorn, situated in the little Karoo, and those in the hot, dry northern Transvaal (grown with irrigation) have done well. At one place near Cape Town, the bushes grew well for four years and suddenly all died, apparently because of a rise in the water table, which flooded the roots.

The first commercial plantings of jojoba were made in 1979, 1980, and 1981. They are all in the Duineveld region, east of Cape Town, and total 850 acres (340 hectares). Moles, deer, and rabbits have caused problems in jojoba plantings in some areas.

Namibia

Jojoba seedlings have been planted in Otjiwarongo. Reportedly, they are doing exceptionally well.

Senegal

A few rows of jojoba plants are surviving with little care and no irrigation in a 23-inch (580 mm) annual rainfall zone at the forestry research station near Bandia.

Morocco

A few plants grown successfully at Marrakesh have been transplanted experimentally to regions along Morocco's southern border.

Other African countries expressing interest in planting jojoba include Algeria, Benin, Cameroon, Cape Verde, Chad, Djibouti, Egypt, Mali, Mauritania, Niger, Nigeria, Somalia, and The Gambia.

Middle East

Israel

The harsh environment of the Negev Desert resembles that of jojoba's homeland, and Israeli scientists have been studying jojoba

APPENDIX A: JOJOBA OUTSIDE NORTH AMERICA

Kalia, Israel. Jojoba growing in saline soils near the Dead Sea. Salinity is one of the greatest constraints to agriculture, and there is an urgent worldwide need for crops that can withstand salt. Jojoba, it seems, can grow in soils of high salinity. (J. Turner)

since the late 1950s. They were the first outside North America to try growing the crop on a relatively large scale, and Israel currently has one of the most significant research programs on jojoba. More than 20 researchers from the Ben-Gurion University of the Negev have studied many aspects of its agronomy and product development.

Much of the early planting in Israel was in experimental plots, aimed at developing and selecting superior plants for large commercial plantations. Between 1977 and 1980, about 200 acres (80 hectares) of jojoba were established for commercial purposes in Hatzerim near Beer-Sheva and in the northern Negev Desert. Today, 30 private jojoba growers in Israel have planted about 1,000 acres (400 hectares) in areas from the driest southern part of the Negev Desert to the verdant shores of the Sea of Galilee in the north.

Most of these areas have been directly sown with seed selected from high-producing local plants. Small areas were planted with vegetatively propagated material. All plantings apply trickle irrigation, employing fresh, sewage, or brackish water. Commercial harvests have already been made in the oldest plantations. Some irrigated and fertilized plants have yielded up to 5.5 pounds (2.5 kg) of fruits per plant. There are some notable specimens growing in a saline region near the Dead Sea.

Israel has a commercial facility that offers for export and local use plantlets tissue cultured from Israel's elite jojoba plants.

Kuwait

A few seedlings planted in the late 1970s, and left without care or watering, indicate that jojoba can survive Kuwait's temperatures, which reach as high as 122°F (50°C) in the shade.

Saudi Arabia

A few, much-neglected specimens indicate that the plant will survive and set fruit near Riyadh.

Turkey

Since 1982 a few plants have been growing well on hillslopes near Adana in southeastern Turkey where summers are hot and dry.

Other countries of the Middle East that have expressed interest in growing jojoba include United Arab Emirates, Yemen (Sanaa), and Yemen (Aden).

Asia

India

In the late 1970s, about 1,500 seedlings were planted by the Central Salt and Marine Chemicals Research Institute at Bhavnagar (Gujarat) on India's west coast and at Behrampur (Orissa) on the east coast. This was the first organized cultivation in the country, and so far the plants are doing well.

At present, there are many small experimental plantations in places such as the National Botanical Garden at Lucknow and the University of Jodhpur at Jodhpur in the Rajasthan Desert.

At Durgapura in Jaipur, 12,000 plants were established in 1981 and first produced seeds 2 years later. The plants are given several waterings during the summer months and one fertilization a year. There have been problems with a biting insect pest and a Rhizoctonia root rot pathogen, but overall the plants are healthy and vigorous.

Europe

Italy

Some 20 acres (8 hectares) of jojoba have been planted on the southern coast of Sardinia using seed from Arizona. Also, about 70 acres (28 hectares) have been established in Calabria, in the southern region of Italy's mainland.

Spain

The Spanish government, through the Institute of Nature Conservation, implemented a jojoba project in 1980. Experimental plots were established mainly in the region of Almeria. The plant has also been planted experimentally near Nijar, Seville, Cordoba, and Amarca. There are some plants in the Canary Islands as well.

Reportedly, in all these sites the plants are acclimatizing well. The total area is about 125 acres (50 hectares) and selections of superior plants are being made with a view to beginning a possible industry. A Spanish jojoba association was established in 1984. Jojoba is seen as a possible crop for diversifying agriculture in the south and southeastern parts.

Other European countries planting trial crops are Greece and Cyprus.

Pacific

Australia

Australia has the capacity to be a big contributor to the world supply of jojoba. During the past decade, state departments of agriculture or forestry as well as the Commonwealth Scientific and Industrial Research Organization (CSIRO) have set up trial nurseries in all the mainland states and in the Northern Territory. The plants are growing in many different environments. For example, CSIRO's Division of Plant Industry has established observational nurseries at locations ranging from Moomba in the South Australian desert to Murwillumbah in a subtropical area near the northern coast of New South Wales.

In Canberra, the CSIRO is also studying jojoba in a controlled environment laboratory. The work aims to find out more about rates of photosynthesis and water use, the factors that induce flower development, environmental factors affecting fruit growth, and propagation methods.

Apart from these government-sponsored programs, private entrepreneurs have begun investing in jojoba plantations. These are located in selected areas of New South Wales, Queensland, South Australia, Victoria, and Western Australia. They range from individual and corporate investments to syndicates. Some plantations have proved highly productive; some have failed. By late 1984 there were about 20 commercial plantations in all, totalling some 5,000 acres (2,000 hectares). The oldest dated from 1978, but the median age was 3-4 years. The planting of improved seed began only in 1984, so most sites have extremely variable plants. In some areas the plants survived the worst drought in Australia's history.

Despite these early developments, the Director-General of Agriculture for the state of New South Wales recently warned that jojoba is still an experimental crop and that potential investors need substantial financial resources if they are to become involved. One particular hazard is that most parts of Australia get some frost.

Jojoba seems notably promising for regions on the periphery of the huge "wheat belt." Frost is light there, and it is thought that strains that can tolerate such conditions can be selected.

New Zealand

Adventurous horticulturists have planted a few jojobas in various parts of the North Island for observation.

Hawaii

Jojoba was first introduced to Hawaii in 1973. Richard Bullock and his students at the University of Hawaii grew the plant at various elevations on several islands as a trial. The most successful was at an elevation of 1,800 feet (600 m) on the island of Maui, where the plants thrived; some have set seed well even in their third year. One entrepreneur is now establishing a commercial plantation. The major problem is that the tropical year-round warmth and sunlight causes year-round flowering, which is undesirable in a crop that is to be machine harvested. It is believed that flowering can be controlled using chemical sprays.

Contacts

The following individuals provided information used in this appendix:

Argentina
Ricardo Ayerza, Technical Advisor, La Magdalena, Cerrito 822 – 7º piso, (1010) Buenos Aires

Australia
Thomas R. Lanny, President, Jojoba Association of Australia, 325 Riley Street, Surry Hills, New South Wales 2010
A. Lennox C. Davidson, Groundwork Pty. Ltd., P.O. Box 124 City, Canberra, A.C.T. 2601
Robert L. Dunstone, Division of Plant Industry, CSIRO, Canberra, A.C.T.
Michael A. Hawson, Department of Agriculture, Jarrah Road, South Perth, Western Australia 6151

Brazil
Gladstone Aragao, Universidade Federal do Ceara, Centro de Ciencias Agrarias, CP 354, Fortaleza, Ceara 60.000

Chile
Waldo Ceron, Facultad de Agronomìa, Universidad Catòlica de Chile, Casilla 114 D, Santiago
Gastón Saint-Jean, Casilla 16055, Santiago 9

Costa Rica
Donald Zeaser, Forestales Asociados S.A., Apartado 146, Moravia

Curaçao
M. van Wilpen, Postbox 853, Curaçao, Netherlands Antilles

Hawaii, USA
Peter M. Amcotts, International Resource and Development Corporation, P.O. Box 2364, Honolulu 96804

India
Central Salt and Marine Chemicals Research Institute, Waghawadi Road, Bhavnagar, 364002 Zanjmer, Gujarat
Department of Botany, University of Jodhpur, Jodhpur, Rajasthan
H. G. Singh, Assistant Plant Pathologist, Agriculture Research Station, Durgapura, Jaipur-302015
National Botanical Research Institute, Rana, Pratap Marg, Lucknow 226001

Israel
Yair Inov, Negev Jojoba Co., P.O.B. 1831, Tel-Aviv 61000

Italy

Giovanni Mignoni, AgipPetroli, Via Laurentina, 449, 00142 Roma

Mexico

Fernando Lubbert A., Guadalupe Victoria y Colima No. 10 – Int. 7, Hermosillo, Sonora
Xicotencatl Murrieta, Secretaría de Desarrollo Urbano y Ecología, Apdo. Postal A-068, Hermosillo, Sonora

Paraguay

Julio G. Spinzi, National Commission for Chaco Development, Edificio Colon 1 Torre 2º piso, Oficina Colon Entre Paraguay Independiente Benjamin Constant, Asunción

Senegal

Claude R. Bailly, Département de Recherches Forestières et Hydrobiologiques, Institute Sénégalais de Recherches Agricoles (ISRA), B.P. 2312, Dakar-Hann

South Africa

Keith Pulvermacher, 14 Hugon Road, Claremont 7700

Spain

Antonio Garcia, Departamento Nacional de Olivicultura y Elaiotecnia, Cordoba

Sudan

Mohamed M. A. Khairi, Department of Horticulture, Ministry of Agriculture, Khartoum
Mahdi Osman El Mardi, Department of Horticulture, Khartoum

Tanzania

Eric Derrickson, P.O. Box 1545, Dar es Salaam

Turkey

Sami Dinkoglu, Ozler Cadsi Kristal Palas, Kat 1 No. 16, Adana

Zimbabwe

William R. Mills, 28 York Avenue, Highlands, Harare

Appendix B
Sources for More Information

The best source of continuing information on jojoba is *Jojoba Happenings*, the official publication of the Jojoba Growers Association. Published bimonthly, this newspaper provides not only information on the latest jojoba developments but also editorials, literature reviews, and advertisements for organizations selling such things as seed, oil, equipment, and land. The annual subscription is $15; $3 per copy. Available from 805 North Fourth Avenue, Suite 404, Phoenix, Arizona 85003, USA. Phone: (602) 253-5470.

Associations

The Jojoba Growers Association is a nonprofit organization of growers, processors, researchers, and suppliers promoting the advancement of the jojoba industry. It holds conferences and symposia and distributes jojoba information, including a membership directory ($10), reprints of a feature article on jojoba from the *Journal of the American Oil Chemists' Society* ($3), and this report. The address is: 3320 East Shea Boulevard, Suite 290, Phoenix, Arizona 85028, USA. Phone: (602) 996-4563.

Other associations devoted to jojoba include:

- The International Jojoba Association, c/o Wm Howard O'Brien, 4350 East Camelback Road, Phoenix, Arizona 85018, USA
- The Jojoba Society of America, c/o T. K. Miwa, 2086 East La Jolla Drive, Tempe, Arizona 85282, USA
- Jojoba Association of Australia, 325 Riley Street, Surry Hills, New South Wales 2010, Australia
- Latin America Association for Jojoba, c/o Ricardo Ayerza, La Magdalena, Cerrito 822 – 7° piso, (1010) Buenos Aires, Argentina
- Texas Jojoba Growers Association, c/o Fred Jordan, 3616 Howell, Dallas, Texas 75204, USA

Literature Services

Jojoba literature is indexed and entered into the AGRICOLA data base (National Agricultural Library). AGRICOLA is available from the Dialog and SDC Orbit System computer database vendors.

The Office of Arid Lands Studies at the University of Arizona (845 North Park Avenue, Tucson, Arizona 85719, USA) maintains a comprehensive collection of jojoba literature, and will provide photocopies of any jojoba-related article. (The cost, in mid-1985, is U.S. 10 cents per page.)

Conference Reports

The proceedings of the Sixth International Conference on Jojoba and its Uses (held in Beer-Sheva, Israel, October 1984) are being prepared. This book will contain more than 50 papers and will be the most up-to-date detailed account of many aspects of jojoba, from agronomy to acne control. (To order, contact J. Wisniak, Department of Chemical Engineering, Ben-Gurion University of the Negev, P.O. Box 653, Beer-Sheva, 84105, Israel.)

Haase, Edward F. and McGinnies, William G., eds. 1972. Jojoba and Its Uses—An International Conference, University of Arizona, June 1972. Available from the Office of Arid Lands Studies, University of Arizona, 845 North Park Avenue, Tucson, Arizona 85719, USA. 81 pages.

Elias-Cesnik, Anna, ed. Jojoba and Its Uses Through 1982. Proceedings of the Fifth International Conference on Jojoba and Its Uses, October 11–15, 1982, Tucson, Arizona. Available from the Office of Arid Lands Studies, University of Arizona.

Bibliographies

Jojoba: Guide to the Literature. 1982. Office of Arid Lands Studies, University of Arizona, Tucson. This 232-page document is a comprehensive guide to the literature on jojoba. It includes: an annotated bibliography citing jojoba-specific research works; a selected bibliography of historical, ethnobotanical, and early taxonomic and systematic literature; a key word index; and full botanical illustrations of the jojoba plant.

This book is available from the Office of Arid Lands Studies for $15 (for air parcel post add $3 Canada/Mexico, or $7 overseas; Arizona residents must add 4 percent sales tax).

All 600 articles in Jojoba: Guide to the Literature are being put on microfiche. Copies of the roughly 1,000 microfiche cards (containing 50,000 pages of text) will be available for purchase from Office of Arid Lands Studies. (Expected availability, September 1985.)

APPENDIX B: SOURCES FOR MORE INFORMATION

Books and Journal Articles

General Reviews

Haumann, B. F. 1983. Jojoba: First harvest of cultivated plantations bringing desert crop closer to widespread commercial use. Journal of the American Oil Chemists' Society 60(1):44-58. Reprints available from Jojoba Growers Association.

Mignoni, G. 1985. La Jojoba. Edagricole, (Via Emilia Levante, 31-Bologna, Italy) 133 pp. (A glossy, large-format book in Italian; contains dozens of color photographs, drawings, diagrams, and maps. Author's address: AgipPetroli, Via Laurentina, 449, 00142 Roma, Italy.)

Natural History

Gentry, H.S. 1958. The natural history of jojoba (*Simmondsia chinensis*) and its cultural aspects. Economic Botany 12(3):261.

Agronomy

Hogan, L. 1979. Jojoba: A new crop for arid regions. Pp. 177–205 in New Agricultural Crops, G. A. Ritchie, ed. AAAS Selected Symposium 38. Westview Press, Boulder, Colorado, USA.

Hogan, L., D. A. Palzkill, and R. E. Dennis. 1981. Production of Jojoba in Arizona. Agricultural Experiment Station Cooperative Extension Service Publication No. 81132. College of Agriculture, The University of Arizona, Tucson, Arizona 85721, USA. 12 pp.

Benge, M. D., ed. 1983. Jojoba: A promising new crop for arid lands. Technical series #14. Available from: S&T/FNR Agro-forestation, Rm. 515D, SA-18, Agency for International Development, Washington, D.C. 20523, USA.

Chemistry

Miwa, T. K., ed. 1980. Jojoba. Volume 1. Fundamental and Applied Research Communications, Notes, Reviews. Jojoba Plantation Products, Inc., Los Angeles, California, USA. 318 pp. (Available from the author at 2086 East La Jolla Drive, Tempe, Arizona 85282, USA.)

Wisniak, J. 1977. Jojoba oil and derivatives. Pp. 167–218 in Progress in the Chemistry of Fats and other Lipids, R. T., Holman, ed. Pergamon Press, Oxford, Great Britain.

Wisniak, J. In press. Chemistry and technology of jojoba oil: State of the art. Proceedings of the Sixth International Conference on Jojoba and Its Uses, 1984. Ben-Gurion University of the Negev, Beer-Sheva, Israel.

Lubricants

Estefan, R. M. 1983. Jojoba as a Possible Lubricant. Paper presented at 74th Annual meeting of the American Oil Chemists' Society, Chicago, Illinois, May 8–12, 1983. (Available from author, Southwest Research Institute, 6220 Culebra Road, San Antonio, Texas 78284, USA.)

Miwa, T. K. and J. A. Rothfus. 1978. In-depth comparison of sulfurized jojoba and sperm whale oils as extreme-pressure/extreme-temperate lubricants. Pp. 243–267 in Proceedings 3rd International Conference on Jojoba, D. M. Yermanos, ed. University of California, Riverside, California.

Cosmetics

Brown, J. H. 1984. Jojoba. A report on the current status of the jojoba industry, including a discussion of several new derivatives that should be of interest to cosmetic formulators. HAPPI, October 1984. Copies available from the author, c/o Jojoba Growers and Processors, Inc., 2267 South Coconino Drive, Apache Junction, Arizona 85220. USA.

Cadicamo, P. and J. Cadicamo. 1982. A study of jojoba oil, its derivatives and other cosmetic oils. Cosmetics and Toiletry 97(2):67–70.
Cadicamo, P. and J. Cadicamo. 1983. A second study of jojoba oil, its derivatives and other cosmetic oils. Soap, Cosmetics, and Chemical Specialties 59(6):36–38.
Libby, H., R. H. Purdy, R. L. Realina, and T. A. Lutgo. In press. Cosmetics based on jojoba oil: I. Oxidation stability. Proceedings of the Sixth International Conference on Jojoba and Its Uses, 1984. Ben-Gurion University of the Negev, Beer-Sheva, Israel.
Shani, A. 1983. Jojoba oil and some of its derivatives in cosmetic health products. Soap, Cosmetics, and Chemical Specialties 59(7):42 & 44.
Taguchi, M. In press. Test results on safety of jojoba alcohol for cosmetic use. Proceedings of the Sixth International Conference on Jojoba and Its Uses, 1984. Ben-Gurion University of the Negev, Beer-Sheva, Israel.

Dermatology

McClatchey, K. 1982. In-vitro antimicrobial effects of jojoba oil. Pp. 289–298 in Proceedings of the Fourth International Conference on Jojoba Oil, Hermosillo, Mexico.
McClatchey, K. 1982. Percutaneous absorption of jojoba oil. Pp. 278–288 in Proceedings of the Fourth International Conference on Jojoba Oil, Hermosillo, Mexico.
Mosovich, B. In press. Treatment of acne and psoriasis. Proceedings of the Sixth International Conference on Jojoba and Its Uses, 1984. Ben-Gurion University of the Negev, Beer-Sheva, Israel.
Yaron, A., A. Benzioni, I. More, and A. Meshorer. In press. Physiological effects of jojoba oil in laboratory animals. Proceedings of the Sixth International Conference on Jojoba and Its Uses, 1984. Ben Gurion University of the Negev, Beer-Sheva, Israel.

Antifoam

Pathak, S. G., R. F. de Philipps, R. M. Kerwin, L. L. Hepler, W. Tien, and H. E. Alburn. 1978. Jojoba oil as an antifoam agent in antibiotic fermentation. Pp. 285–290 in La Jojoba. Consejo Nacional de Ciencia y Tecnologia, Insurgentes Sur 1677, Z.P. 20, D. F. Mexico City, Mexico.

Food

Bizzi, A., M. Cini, and U. Bracco. In press. Absorption and distribution of jojoba oil after oral administration to rats. Proceedings of the Sixth International Conference on Jojoba and Its Uses, 1984. Ben-Gurion University of the Negev, Beer-Sheva, Israel.
Decombaz, J., C. Heise, and K. Anantharaman. In press. Nutritional investigations on jojoba (*Simmondsia chinensis*) oil. Proceedings of the Sixth International Conference on Jojoba and Its Uses, 1984. (See above.)

Wax

Miwa, T. K. 1978. Hardness test for wax formulations from jojoba wax, paraffin, polythylene, and polypropylene. Pp. 265–274 in La Jojoba. Consejo Nacional de Ciencia y Tecnologia, Insurgentes Sur 1677, Z.P. 20, D. F. Mexico City, Mexico.

Detoxification of Seed Meal

Storey, R., N. Bower, C. V. Lovejoy, and R. Taggart. 1982. Analysis of selected nutritional and anti-nutritional factors in jojoba seed from the United States and Mexico. Pp. 21–31 in Jojoba and Its Uses Through 1982, Proceedings of the Fifth International Conference, Anna Elias-Cesnik, ed. University of Arizona, Tucson, Arizona.

APPENDIX B: SOURCES FOR MORE INFORMATION

Verbiscar, J. A. and T. A. Banigan. 1982. Jojoba meal as a livestock feed. Pp. 267–280 in Jojoba and Its Uses Through 1982, Proceedings of the Fifth International Conference, Anna Elias-Cesnik, ed. University of Arizona, Tucson, Arizona.

Weber, C. W., J. W. Berry, and E. M. Cook. 1982. Influence of jojoba meal upon growth and reproduction in mice. Pp. 93–99 in Jojoba and Its Uses Through 1982, Proceedings of the Fifth International Conference, Anna Elias-Cesnik, ed. University of Arizona, Tucson, Arizona.

Jojoba in the United States

Yermanos, D. M. 1979. Jojoba—a crop whose time has come. California Agriculture 33(718):4–11.

Yermanos, D. M. 1982. Performance of jojoba under cultivation between 1973–1982: Information developed at the University of California, Riverside. Pp. 197–211 in Jojoba and Its Uses Through 1982, Proceedings of the Fifth International Conference, Anna Elias-Cesnik, ed. University of Arizona, Tucson, Arizona.

Jojoba in Australia

Davidson, S. 1983. Jojoba: cautious optimism. Rural Research 119:21–25.

Hawson, M. G. 1984. Jojoba in Western Australia. Department of Agriculture, Perth, Western Australia.

Jojoba in Latin America

Aragao, R. G. M. and D. C. Monteiro. 1982. A cultura da jojoba no Nordeste do Brasil. Banco do Nordeste do Brasil S.A., Rua Senador Pompeu, 590, 60.000, Fortaleza, Ceara, Brasil.

Ayerza, R. 1984. La Jojoba. Editorial Hemisferio sur S.A. Buenos Aires, Argentina. 224 pp. (Copies available from author at La Magdalena, Cerrito 822 − 7º piso, (1010) Buenos Aires, Argentina.)

Appendix **C**

Contributors to the Study

Peter M. Amcotts, International Research and Development Corporation, P.O. Box 2364, Honolulu, Hawaii 96804, USA
Steve Anderson, Cargill Corporation, P.O. Box 9300, Minneapolis, Minnesota 55440, USA
Gladstone Aragao, Universidade Federal do Ceara, Centro de Ciencias Agrarias, CP 354, Fortaleza, Ceara 60.000, Brazil
Ricardo Ayerza, Technical Advisor, La Magdalena, Cerrito 822 – 7° piso, (1010) Buenos Aires, Argentina
Arne Belsby, Jojoba Enterprises, Inc., P.O. Box 396, Desert Center, California 92239, USA
Hanoch Benajahu, Ben-Gurion University of the Negev, P.O. Box 653, Beer-Sheva 84105, Israel
Taye Bezuneh, Department of Plant Science, University of Arizona, Tucson, Arizona 85721, USA
Aliza Benzioni, Ben-Gurion University of the Negev, P.O. Box 653, Beer-Sheva 84105, Israel
Eliott Birnbaum, Institute of Applied Research, Ben-Gurion University of the Negev, P.O. Box 1025, Beer-Sheva 84110, Israel
Hugh Bollinger, Director, NPI, Inc., 417 Wakara Way, Salt Lake City, Utah 84108, USA
U. Bracco, Nestlé Products Technical Assistance Company, Case Postale 88, CH-1814 La Tour de Peilz, Switzerland
James H. Brown, Jojoba Growers and Processors Inc., 2267 South Coconino Drive, Apache Junction, Arizona 85220, USA
Waldo Ceron, Facultad de Agronomía, Universidad Católica de Chile, Casilla 114 D, Santiago, Chile
A. Lennox C. Davidson, Groundwork Pty. Ltd., P.O. Box 124 City, Canberra, A.C.T. 2601, Australia
Jacques Décombaz, Research Department, Nestlé, Case Postale 88, CH-1814 La Tour de Peilz, Switzerland
Robert L. Dunstone, Division of Plant Industry, CSIRO, Canberra, Australia
Kelley Dwyer, Executive Director, Jojoba Growers and Processors Inc., 2267 South Coconino Drive, Apache Junction, Arizona 85220, USA
Gordon Fisher, Agrifuture Inc., 3651 Pegasus Drive, Suite 101, Bakersfield, California 93308, USA
William Feldman, Director, Boyce Thompson Southwestern Arboretum, P.O. Box AB, Superior, Arizona 85273, USA
Meir Forti, Institute of Applied Research, Ben-Gurion University of the Negev, P.O. Box 1025, Beer-Sheva 84110, Israel
Howard Scott Gentry, Gentry Experimental Farm, 37100 Los Alamos Road, Murrieta, California 92362, USA.
R. Guidoux, Research Department, Nestec Ltd., CH-1800 Vevey, Switzerland
Sir Rupert Hamer, Jojoba Management Limited, Southport, Queensland, Australia
LeMoyne Hogan, Plant Sciences Department, University of Arizona, Tucson, Arizona 85721, USA
Yair Inov, Negev Jojoba Co., P.O.B. 1831, Tel-Aviv 61000, Israel
Amram (Ron) Kadish, Agricultural Consultant, AG Associates, 1980 Hobart Drive, Camarillo, California 93010, USA

APPENDIX C: CONTRIBUTORS TO THE STUDY

Lawrence R. Knowles, Southwest Jojoba Company, 4325 West Shaw Avenue, Fresno, California 93711, USA
Phillip S. Landis, Glassboro State College, Glassboro, New Jersey 08028, USA
Thomas R. Lanny, President, Jojoba Association of Australia, 325 Riley Street, Surry Hills, New South Wales 2010, Australia
Chi Won Lee, Department of Plant Sciences, University of Arizona, Tucson, Arizona 85721, USA
Henry Libby, Libby Laboratories Inc., 1700 Sixth Street, Berkeley, California 94710, USA
Lourdes A. Lizarrage, (CICTUS) University of Sonora, Hermosillo, Sonora, Mexico
Fernando Lubbert A., Guadalupe Victoria y Colima No. 10 – Int. 7, Hermosillo, Sonora, Mexico
Cyrus McKell, Vice President, Research, NPI, Inc., 417 Wakara Way, Salt Lake City, Utah 84108, USA
Kenneth D. McLatchey, Department of Pathology, University of Michigan Medical School, Ann Arbor, Michigan 48109–0010, USA
Roland A. Manolo, So-Cal Jojoba, 891 Navajo Drive, Riverside, California 92507, USA
William P. Miller, Amerind Agrotech Laboratory, Sacaton, Arizona 85247, USA
Kay Mirocha, Office of Arid Lands Studies, University of Arizona, Tucson, Arizona 85719, USA
Thomas Miwa, 2086 East La Jolla Drive, Tempe, Arizona 85282, USA
Bernardo Mosovich, Soroka Medical Center, Ben-Gurion University of the Negev, Beer-Sheva 84105, Israel
Walter B. Mors, Instituto de Ciencias Biomedicas, Universidade Federal do Rio de Janeiro, Dept. de Bioquimica, ZC32, Rio de Janeiro, Brazil
B. Thomas Morring, Indio, California 92201, USA
Daniel A. Murray, Jojoba Plantation Partners, Santa Paula, California 93060, USA
Xicotencatl Murrieta, Secretaria de Desarrollo Urbano y Ecología, Apdo. Postal A-068, Hermosillo, Sonora, Mexico
Karl J. Niklas, Department of Plant Science, Cornell University, Ithaca, New York, 14853, USA
William H. O'Brien, O'Brien Industries, 4350 East Camelback Road, Phoenix, Arizona 85018, USA
David A. Palzkill, Plant Sciences Department, University of Arizona, Tucson, Arizona 85721, USA
S. G. Pathak, Fermenta Products, Inc., West Chester, Pennsylvania 19382, USA
Bernard Pompeo, President, Frank B. Ross Co., Inc., P.O. Box 4085, Jersey City, New Jersey 07304–0085, USA
Ralph L. Price, Department of Nutrition and Food Science, University of Arizona, Tucson, Arizona 85721, USA
Hal C. Purcell, McVay Jojoba Co., 142 Front Street, Avila Beach, California 93424, USA
Steve Reddy, Plant Science Department, University of Arizona, Tucson, Arizona 85721, USA
Rudolf Schmid, Department of Botany, University of California, Berkeley, California, 94720, USA
Arnon Shani, Ben-Gurion University of the Negev, P.O. Box 653, Beer-Sheva 84105, Israel
Lee St. Lawrence, 388 London Road, Deal, Kent CT14 9PR, England
Rolf Stalder, Research Department, Nestec Ltd., CH-1800 Vevey, Switzerland
Robert Stryker, P.O. Box 1535, Florence, Arizona 85232, USA
Masayuki Taguchi, Koei-Perfumery Company, Ltd., Tokyo, Japan
Robert F. Thorne, Rancho Santa Ana Botanic Garden, Claremont, California 91711, USA
Anthony J. Verbiscar, President, Anver Bioscience Design, Inc., 160 East Monticito Avenue, Sierra Madre, California 91024, USA
Carole Ann Whittaker, President, The Jojoba Growers Association, 3320 East Shea Boulevard, Suite 290, Phoenix, Arizona 85003, USA

Jaime Wisniak, Department of Chemical Engineering, Ben-Gurion University of the Negev, P.O. Box 653, Beer-Sheva 84105, Israel

Demetrios M. Yermanos, Department of Agronomy, University of California, Riverside, California (deceased)

Mohamed H. Younez, Tenneco West, P.O. Box 9380, Bakersfield, California 93309, USA

Donald Zeaser, Forestales Asociados S.A., Apartado 146, Moravia, Costa Rica

Advisory Committee on Technology Innovation

ELMER L. GADEN, JR., Department of Chemical Engineering, University of Virginia, Charlottesville, Virginia, *Chairman*

Members

RAYMOND C. LOEHR, Director, Environmental Studies Program, Cornell University, Ithica, New York
CYRUS M. MCKELL, NPI, Inc., Salt Lake City, Utah
DONALD L. PLUCKNETT, Consultative Group on International Agricultural Research, Washington, D.C.
EUGENE B. SHULTZ, JR., Professor of Engineering and Applied Science, Washington University, St. Louis, Missouri

Board on Science and Technology for International Development

RALPH H. SMUCKLER, Dean of International Studies and Programs, Michigan State University, East Lansing, Michigan, *Chairman*

Members

SAMUEL P. ASPER, President, Educational Commission for Foreign Medical Graduates, Washington, D.C.
DAVID BELL, Department of Population Sciences, Harvard School of Public Health, Boston, Massachusetts
LAWRENCE L. BOGER, President, Oklahoma State University, Stillwater, Oklahoma
ROBERT H. BURRIS, Department of Biochemistry, University of Wisconsin, Madison, Wisconsin
NATE FIELDS, Director, Developing Markets, Control Data Corporation, Edina, Minnesota
ELMER L. GADEN, JR., Department of Chemical Engineering, University of Virginia, Charlottesville, Virginia
JOHN H. GIBBONS, Director, U.S. Congress, Office of Technology Assessment, Washington, D.C.
ADELAIDE CROMWELL GULLIVER, Brookline, Massachusetts
WILLIAM HUGHES, Director, Engineering Energy Laboratory, Oklahoma State University, Stillwater, Oklahoma
GEORGE I. LYTHCOTT, University of Wisconsin School of Medicine, Madison, Wisconsin
FREDERICK C. ROBBINS, President, Institute of Medicine, National Academy of Sciences, *ex officio*

WALTER A. ROSENBLITH, Foreign Secretary, National Academy of Sciences, *ex officio*
FREDERICK SEITZ, President Emeritus, the Rockefeller University, New York, *ex officio*
H. GUYFORD STEVER, Foreign Secretary, National Academy of Engineering
BARBARA WEBSTER, Associate Dean, Office of Research, University of California, Davis, California
ALBERT WESTWOOD, Corporate Director, Research and Development, Martin-Marietta Corporation, Bethesda, Maryland
GILBERT F. WHITE, Institute of Behavioral Science, University of Colorado, Boulder, Colorado, *ex officio*
EDWARD O. WILSON, Museum of Comparative Zoology, The Agassiz Museum, Harvard University, Cambridge, Massachusetts

JOHN G. HURLEY, Director
MICHAEL G. C. MCDONALD DOW, Associate Director/Studies
MICHAEL P. GREENE. Associate Director/Research Grants

www.ingramcontent.com/pod-product-compliance
Lightning Source LLC
Chambersburg PA
CBHW021146230426
43667CB00005B/268